A Concise Dictionary
of Cornish Place-Names

A Concise Dictionary
of Cornish Place-Names

Craig Weatherhill

evertype

2009

Published by Evertype, Cnoc Sceichín, Leac an Anfa, Cathair na Mart, Co. Mhaigh Eo, Éire. *www.evertype.com*.

Editor: Michael Everson.

A catalogue record for this book is available from the British Library.

ISBN-10 1-904808-22-0
ISBN-13 978-1-904808-22-0

Typeset in Baskerville by Michael Everson.

Cover design by Michael Everson. The map is by Robert Morden, from *The New Description and State of England, containing the Maps of the Counties of England and Wales, in Fifty Three Copper-Plates, Newly Design'd, Exactly Drawn and Engraven by the best Artists*, London, 1701.

Printed and bound by LightningSource.

Contents

Preface

Many people first take an interest in the Cornish language because they are curious to learn more about the distinctive and fascinating place names of Cornwall.

The key to understanding the meaning of these place-names is language. Most derive from the Cornish language primarily, but many of them have their roots in Old English, Middle English, French, and other languages which have left their mark on Cornwall. Through the tireless and exacting work of place-name specialists, the secrets of Cornish place-names are being unlocked for everyone. This dictionary offers in a concise format more than 3,300 place-names. It is the fruit of Craig Weatherhill's many years of research, not only of the meaning of the names themselves, but of considering the question of how best to represent those names in Revived Cornish. The recommendations in this dictionary preserve the authentic and attested linguistic forms while at the same time honouring the traditional orthographic forms which have been visible on the Cornish landscape for at least four centuries.

The orthography used in this dictionary is compatible with the Standard Written Form (SWF), adopted by the Cornish Language Partnership for educational and official use. It is also compatible with Kernowek Standard (KS), a practical orthography which informed the development of the SWF. In turn, KS has been modified in light of the published SWF specification, while adopting a few emendations to make the orthography more consistent and more like the spelling of traditional Cornish.

As with all such works, this dictionary will doubtless contain errors, however hard its author and editor have striven to avoid them. The book could be larger, reversed, contain maps or Ordnance Survey grid references, or be expanded in other ways. Nevertheless we have published this material in concise form to make available for the first time authentic and traditional names suitable for modern use.

Michael Everson
Westport, Co. Mayo

Introduction

In my work on place-names I have proceeded on the basis of the following definition:

> An historical place-name is one which was firmly established before 1904; the publication date of Henry Jenner's *Handbook of the Cornish Language,* and generally accepted as the commencement of the revival of the Cornish language.

The way in which this working definition has been implemented involves making a number of choices, when evaluating the historically-attested names and normalizing them in the light of standard orthography in Revived Cornish, whilst respecting at the same time the familiar and traditional spellings even of their anglicized forms. Of course this work is not done in a vacuum, and the work of other place-name specialists has informed many of the choices made.

One major source of place-name history is the pair of unpublished manuscripts *The Place-Names of Cornwall* compiled in 1948 by J. E. B. Gover; these being lodged at the Royal Institution of Cornwall, River Street, Truro. This valuable work has been relied upon by many over several decades.

However, Oliver Padel has been at considerable pains to point out that the Gover manuscripts are replete with error, with some historical forms attributed to wrong locations and, therefore, Gover can no longer be regarded as reliable. The task of checking each of Gover's entries against his cited sources is a mammoth one which Padel himself has now undertaken with a view to producing a corrected edition. This work is likely to take several months, if not longer and, with this in mind, a number of names in the appended list might need to be reviewed in the future.

To prepare a dictionary of place-names suitable for the practice of translating toponyms in Cornwall and Scilly for purposes of signage, cartography and use in the Cornish language itself, prime consideration should be given to protecting the historical integrity of each name, be it of Cornish or non-Cornish origin. A number of elements involved in that process are listed here:

Unassibilated Old Cornish elements

In East Cornwall, Old Cornish features remain in numerous place-names, notably the unsoftened word endings such as **nant** (later **nans**) 'valley'; **bod** (later **bos**) 'dwelling', and **cuit** (later **coys** and **coos**) 'a wood'. I recommend that these names from East Cornwall should not be subjected to modern assibilation, because to do so would imply a history that a name did not undergo. It is better to treat these words according to their genuine history: they remained "fossilized" from a period during which the Cornish language became moribund as a community tongue, perhaps in the 12th century or before. The *Old Cornish Vocabulary*, thought to date from about 1200, shows assibilation in some words but not others and, therefore, seems to have been compiled when this process was underway and when the language was in transition.

Exceptions can be made in accordance with historical record. If this shows assibilation in even one recorded example of a place-name, and even though the form in which that name is seen today retains the Old Cornish feature, then reproducing the name in Middle Cornish form should be considered acceptable. Well-known examples are **Bodmin** (*Bosvena* C18) and **Liskeard** (*Lyskerrys* C14).

In West Cornwall, assibilation of a generic element is prevented by the initial **r-** of a qualifying element. For example, one finds **Bodrifty**, **Bodriggy**, and **Redruth** where **Bos-** and either **Res-** or **Rys-** might have been expected. This feature should remain and not undergo "correction" to an assibilated form.

Pre-occlusion

This feature of Late Cornish development places an intrusive **b** before **m**, and **d** before **n**, in a stressed syllable, so that **penn** (*pen*, 'head, top, end') becomes **pedn**, and **tomm** ('warm') becomes **tobm**. It is found in many place-names in the western half of Cornwall within which its use was restricted (the easternmost toponym containing pre-occlusion appears to be in the parish of St Ewe). This feature represents a genuine linguistic development and should, naturally be included in modern recommended spellings. I do however recommend that pre-occlusion should only be used where attested in the historical record for an individual name; it is best not to introduce it where it did not historically occur.

The alternation s~j

A further late feature in Western Cornwall was the replacement of **s** by **j** in words such as *gwynjek* (Middle Cornish *gwynsek*), 'windy'. Again, where this development can be shown to have historically occurred, it should be observed in recommended spellings—but it should not be introduced where it did not occur.

Initial mutation

Ths feature, which is common to all Celtic languages, is shown by the grammars to occur under specific rules and conditions. Place-names, however, are notoriously inconsistent with regard to mutation, often omitting it where it is expected, or applying it where it "should not" occur.

When reconstructing Cornish place-names for road-signs, cartography, and so on, should mutation be applied strictly in accordance with the linguistic rules, or left alone? Are there, in fact, reasons for some of the inconsistencies that are not, as yet, fully understood?

My recommendation is that, in the case of historic place-names, the vagaries of initial mutation be left alone and that each name be dealt with in accordance with its own history.

For example, *eglos* 'church', a feminine singular noun, should cause lenition according to the rules—but, in fact, rarely does. It is felt that this merits respect and qualifiers should not have lenition introduced to them.

Provection often occurs in qualifiers following an generic that ends with -s, as in **Nanpean** (*nans + bian*) and **Rospannel** (*ros + banadhel*). This, too, should be retained where it occurs.

Chy- and Ty-

It is generally accepted that *chy* 'house' was the Middle Cornish reflex of Old Cornish *ty*, with occurrence of *chy* commencing *c.* 1200. However, a number of place-names retained the older form, among them **Tehidy**, **Tywardreath**, **Tywarnhayle**, **Tybesta**, and **Degembris**; these locations were major manorial centres. It would seem that retention of the older **Ty** form might have carried a degree of status or prestige. I consider it, therefore, essental that **Ty** in these names should be safeguarded and not converted to **Chy**.

Saints' names

Saints' names are of particular note in Cornish toponyms and the standards of historical representation have been fully detailed by Nicholas Williams in his paper "'Saint' in Cornish" (*Cornish Studies* 7, 1999; reprinted in *Writings on Revived Cornish*, Evertype 2006). In summary, the names of Celtic saints and certain other well-known or apostolic saints, including **Michael** and **John**, are rarely, if ever, preceded by the title "Saint" (**Sent, Sen**) in the language or in historic Cornish forms of place-names. **St Piran**, for example, would not been ***Sen Peran***, but **Peran** or **Peran Sans** ('holy Peran') However, the title was occasionally used in the case of foreign or non-Celtic saints. For example the village of **St Hilary** (Bishop Hilarius of Poitiers) was referred to as *Seynt Eler* c. 1680, but the town of **St Austell** was *Austol* c.1150.

I recommend that the use or non-use of **sen** or **sent** be applied in accordance with the historical record.

Personal names

The original form of personal names contained within place-names is often difficult to determine and it is therefore recommended that these be reproduced in accordance with recorded historical spellings. The name of **St Piran** is, in the vast majority of attested spellings for several place-names, spelt **Peran**, and it is felt that this should be the standard form, rather than the unattested ***Pyran***. The personal name **Sylvester** (adopted from Latin) occurs in three toponyms and, in each case, the first vowel is consistently shown in historic forms as **-a-** (i.e. **Salvester**), this vowel surviving even into the modern form of each name. It is strongly recommended that, in these instances, **Sylvester** be spelt **Salvester**.

Names of non-Cornish origin

The question of whether to translate names of non-Cornish origin into Cornish is a contentious one and will invite a great deal of discussion. The recommendations in this dictionary are firmly grounded in the principle of the preservation of historical integrity, and I believe that this principle should extend to all toponyms, regardless of the language from which they are derived.

Most non-Cornish place-names within the Duchy are English, and are accompanied by a number that have French, or Norman-French origins, and even one, **Collorian**, which is suspected of being coined from classical Greek. Rare names of Scandinavian origin appear to be restricted to the Isles of Scilly. Those of French origin may well date from the centuries of Norman administration before the reinstatement of English as an official tongue, roughly 1100 to 1400. Names of English origin may not have been introduced in Cornwall until the 10th or 11th century.

There are particular problems with translating Old English elements into Cornish. For example, attempts to convert English *stów* 'holy place' names into Cornish *lan* 'early church enclosure', are inappropriate as the Cornish word refers to a particular type of archaeological structure that is rarely found at a *stów* site. A *stów* is not a *lan*.

Similar problems have occurred with Old English *léah* names. This word has been assumed to mean 'a wood' or 'grove', and translated accordingly. However, by the time the Old English word had reached Cornwall, its meaning had altered from 'a wood' to 'clearing'.

A serious mistake of long standing has been the translation of **Torpoint** as ***Pentor*** or ***Penntor***. The original coinage of this Cornish translation is probably half a century old but it misunderstood the derivation of the English name which is a tautology and does not contain the word *tor*. It is, in fact, a contraction of *Stertpoynt* (1608), which consists of Old English *steort* 'tail, promontory', with the addition of a later word which also means 'promontory, headland'. In cases such as this, it may be better to abandon translation (although the alteration of just one letter, to ***Pentir*** 'promontory', would rectify the initial error in this instance).

Nor is it felt that translation of non-Cornish names into Cornish is appropriate when those names were coined after the demise of Cornish in their particular locations. Names such as **Leedstown**, **Townshend**, **Bugle**, and **London Apprentice** were all coined in the 19th century, and these examples contain important historical information that would be obscured by translation (**Leedstown** founded by the Duke of Leeds;

Townshend named after a land-owning St Aubyn married a member of the Townsend family; **Bugle** named after a public house; **London Apprentice** named after a former public house that was, in turn, named after a folk-song). Indeed, could one translate **London Apprentice** into Cornish (*Prentys Loundres*?) without the risk of it bordering on absurdity?

Some have suggested that long-standing translations of English names into Cornish, such as *Aberfal* for **Falmouth** and *Aberplymm* for **Plymouth** are now so well-established that they should be allowed to remain, even though the element *aber* does not historically feature in Cornish place-names. This horse may have bolted from the barn, but I would at least recommend a small alteration of *Aberfal* to *Aberfala*, as the river name tends to be *Fala* in historical record (e.g. toponyms such as *Coysfala* 1337 and *Penfenten fala* 1320).

Translation of non-Cornish names into Cornish is replete with pitfalls such as those mentioned above and is, for the most part, a practice that should be avoided unless the settlement or location is known to have had a recorded Cornish alternative. In this way **Padstow** can safely be presented as *Lanwedhenek*, **Newmills** (Ladock) as *Melynnowyth* and **Newbridge** (Sancreed) as *Hal an Tegen*. In some cases, non-Cornish names have been respelt on the appended list to bring them closer to their own original forms.

In the case of hybrid Cornish-English names, it may be reasonably argued that the Cornish element represents the original name, so that **Caradon** (*Carnedun* c. 1160: Cornish *carn*, "tor" + Old English *dún*, "hill") can be reconstructed as the simplex *Carn*.

Use of apostrophes

Apostrophes occur in several names on the appended list of recommendations, largely in names such as **Tywarnhayle** (*Ty war'n heyl*), which contains a consistently abbreviated definite article, and names such as those with *Bos-*, *Bod-*, "dwelling" where the historical record shows a consistent shortening of the generic element (for example **Botallack** and **Bohetherick**, which are recommended as *Bo'talek* and *Bo'hydrek* respectively).

In some place-names, an apostrophe is used to indicate that there is a hiatus between final **-s** of one syllable and initial **h-** of the next (as opposed to the single sound **sh**): **Retallack** and **Retallick** are written *Res'helyk*, and **Retire** is written *Res'hir*.

Use of hyphens

Hyphens have been used only at line-breaks in the recommended forms; when written out in full there should be no hyphens, particularly on public signage. Hyphens used in anglicized names have been kept without change, however.

Names of uncertain or unknown derivation

A significant number of Cornish toponyms have unknown or, at best, uncertain derivations; **Selena** (St Buryan) and **Caerhayes** (St Michael Caerhayes) being just two examples of names that continue to baffle researchers, despite a wealth of early spellings.

It is recommended that, in cases such as these, assumption be avoided and that a selection be made from the list of historically recorded spellings of each name.

Division of elements

Where to separate place-name elements and where to divide them is not always easy to decide. In most of the historical names the elements are all run together. Some have recommended that Cornish place-names should be divided in line with similar practice in Wales and Ireland. In this dictionary I have tended to leave unstressed prefixes (such as *Lan-*, *Pen-*, *Res-*, *Ros-*, *Tre-*, and *Trev-*) attached, but have separated *Bal*, *Chy*, *Crug*, *Eglos*, *Ker*, and *Ty*. Where the name following *Trev-* begins with a vowel, these too have been separated, to distinguish them from *Tre-* + a mutated following element (compare **Treverbyn**, *Trev Erbyn*, 'Erbin's farm' with **Treverbyn**, *Treverwyn*, 'Berwyn's farm'). Place-names which contain an article or preposition are also separated: **Marazanvose**, *Marhas an Vos*, 'market at the wall'; **Trendrennen**, *Tre'n Dreynen*, 'farm at the thorn bush'; **Tywarnhayle**, *Ty war'n Heyl*, 'manorial centre by tidal flats'.

Division of elements within reconstructed toponyms is a matter for debate and further discussion may be considered appropriate.

Differences from the Standard Written Form

- In every instance the SWF's Traditional Forms have been used, as in **carn**, **coos**, **cudyn**, **whel**.

- The unstressed prefixes **Pen-**, **Lan-**, and **Cam-** are written with a single final letter to ensure that they are not incorrectly pre-occluded by speakers who do pre-occlude stressed **Penn** as **Pedn**, **Lann** as **Ladn**, and **Camm** as **Cabm**.

- Where initial *f-* is mutated to *v-*, the mutation is written, as in **Dowr an Velynjy** 'Valency', **Ker Veynek** 'Carvinack', **Penventynnyow** 'Penventinue'.

- Where initial *s-* is mutated to *z-*, the mutation is written as an option, as in **Coyt Senar~Zenar** 'Zennor Quoit', **Pensans~Penzans** 'Penzance'.

- In a few personal names, **au** has been used rather than **o**, as in **Austol** and **Maunan**. The same has been done for the place-name elements **cauns** 'paved road' and **dauns** 'dance'. The forms **Ostel*, **Monan*, **cons*, and **dons* are too greatly removed from the historical names and traditional pronunciation.

- In a few personal names, **ai** has been used rather than **e**, as in **Caina** 'Kayna', **Mail** 'Mael', **Mailek** 'Maeloc', and **Mailgi** 'Maelgi'. The same has been done for the river **Lain** 'Layne'.

- The SWF distinguishes between three kinds of monosyllables:

  - those which have an alternation in [i] or [əi], written in SWF *-i* or *-ei* (as in **chi~chei** 'house', **dri~drei** 'bring', **gwri~gwrei** 'seam', **gwi~gwei** 'weaves', **hi~hei** 'she', **ki~kei** 'dog', **ni~nei** 'we', **ri~rei** 'give', **tri~trei** 'three' **ti~tei** 'oath', and **i~(anj)ei** 'they')

  - those which end in [i], written in SWF *-y* (as in **bry** 'value', **fy** 'fie', **ly** 'lunch', and **ny** 'not')

  - those ending in [i] or [e], written in SWF *-y* or *-e* (as in **my~me** 'I', and **ty~te** 'you') .

This fine distinction between these three classes of words seems to be quite unnecessary given their small number, and in light of the overwhelming preponderance of **-y** forms in the traditional place-names, as well as in modern house-names, **Ty** and **Chy** have been preferred here. In a few names the SWF's Late Cornish option has been retained, however, as in **Pedn Kei**.

- For the diphthong [iʊ] the spelling **yw** has been preferred to the spelling **iw** which the SWF uses in a handful of words which have *-iw* or *-iv* in Welsh and Breton. Thus this dictionary writes **lyw** 'colour', **nywl** 'mist' rather than **liw*, **niwl*.

- In unstressed final syllables, **-th** has been used in favour of **-dh**, as in **nowyth** 'new', **meneth** 'mountain', **pibyth** 'piper'. (Note that the word for 'mountain' is given as **meneth**, pl. **menydhyow**, as it is in the traditional sources.)

- In unstressed final syllables the traditional **y** has often been preferred to "etymological" **i** which the SWF appears to use. Thus this dictionary writes **melyn** 'mill' (despite Latin *molina*), **elyn** 'elbow', **eythyn** 'furze', **kerdhyn** 'rowan', **kenyn** 'garlic'. This makes final stressed syllables in **-din/-dhin** 'fortress' more obvious.

- The words for 'yellow' and 'owl' are given as **melen** and **ula** as is traditional.

Differences from Kernowek Standard

- The [æː]~[ɑː] alternation is not uniformly marked with **â**. While the SWF writes 'large' as either **bras** or **broas**, KS writes both as **brâs** (distinguished from **bras** 'treachery'); thus **Carn Broas** 'Carn Bras', **Pedn Broas** 'Pednbrose', and **Crug Broas** 'Creegbrawse' are written where KS writes **Brâs** for either pronunciation. The recommended spelling for **Clodgie Point** is **Pedn Cla'jy**, which might be written **Pedn Cloa'jy** in the Late Variant of the SWF, but in KS would be unambigiously **Pedn Clâ'jy** (for **Pedn Clâvjy**).

- The [iː]~[eː] alternation is not uniformly marked with **ÿ~ë**. While the SWF writes 'corn' as either **ys** or **es**, KS distinguishes **ÿs~ës** [iːz]~[eːz] from words like **bys** [bɪz] 'but' and **res** [reːz] 'necessary' (which has no

*[riːz] form). Thus **Men Ys**, 'Maenease Point' and **Porth Ysek** 'Port Isaac', are written here where KS writes **Men Ÿs**, and **Porth Ÿsek**.

- The long vowel [uː] is not distinguished with a diacritic **û** as it is in KS, so **Rumon y'n Woon** 'Ruan Minor' and **Trev Ula**, 'Trefula' are written where KS writes **Rûmon i'n Woon** and **Trev Ûla**.

- The preposition 'in' is written **yn**, where KS writes **in**, as in **Rumon y'n Woon**, 'Ruan Minor', **Carrek Loos y'n Coos** 'St Michael's Mount', where KS would have **i'n** 'in the'.

Notwithstanding the departures from the Standard Written Form and Kernowek Standard orthographies detailed above, which are necessitated by the requirement to retain historical integrity, I would like to emphasize that the forms recommended for modern use remain compatible with both. I would like to acknowledge the support of the Cornish Language Development office, which encouraged me to prepare a list of recommendations of historic place-names for modern use.

Much of the detail in this dictionary results from discussion with a number of experts in linguistics and toponymy. In this regard, I wish to thank, in particular, Nicholas Williams, Michael Everson, Eddie Forbeis Climo, Oliver Padel, Andrew Climo, Charles Thomas, as well as the late P. A. S. Pool. For what errors may yet persist, I bear the final responsibility alone; but I trust that this book will still be useful and interesting despite any imperfections.

Craig Weatherhill

Hal an Tegen, Pensans

January 2009

Abbreviations

C15 etc.	15th century
Cor.	Cornish
D	Dutch
E	English
F	French
Gk	Greek
L	Latin
LC	Late Cornish
ME	Middle English
MF	Middle French
OC	Old Cornish
OE	Old English
OF	Old French
OS	Ordnance Survey
O.Sc	Old Scandinavian

Cornwall and the Isles of Scilly

Cornwall (*Kernow* C14), Kernow, ?*'promontory people'*

Scilly, Isles of (*Sillan c.* 1680), Syllan, ?*'place sacred to the goddess Sulis'*

Hundreds, regions, etc.

Brannel (*Branel* 1201), Bronel, *'place of hills'*

East Wivelshire (*Rileston* 1084), Ryslegh, *'manor of Rillaton'*

Kerrier (*Keryer c.* 1230–1484), Keryer, *'place of forts'*

Lesnewth (*Lysnewyth* 1238), Lysnowyth, *'new court'*

Meneage (*Manahec* 1269), Manahek, *'monastic land'*

North Cornwall (*an Tereathe Euhall* C17), an Tireth Uhel, *'the high region'*

Penwith (*Penwyth* 1236), Penwyth, *'end district'*

Powder (*Poureder* 1131), Pow Ereder, *'ploughland region'*

Pydar (*Piderscire* 1131), Pedera, *'fourth (Hundred)'*

Rame Peninsula (*Ros c.* 710), Ros, *'promontory'*

Roseland (*Ros* 1259), Ros, *'promontory'*

Stratton (*Straetneat c.* 881), Stradneth (OC), *'valley of river Neth'*

Trigg (*Tricorscire c.* 881), Trigor', Trigordh, *'three hosts'*

West Wivelshire (*Fawiton* 1084), Fowy, *'manor of Fawiton'*

Rivers, estuaries, & lakes

Note In line with traditional Cornish place name practice, *dowr* is used to denote 'river'. However, some names include an archaic -*y* river name suffix (and, in one case, OE -*éa*). In order to avoid tautology, *dowr* is not added in these names.

Allen (*Layne* 1466, *c.* 1540), Dowr Lain, (?*meaning*)

Amble (*Amal* 1086, 1306), Dowr Amal, *'boundary river'*

Antron (*Anter* 1266), Dowr Anter, (?*meaning*)

Bude (*Bedewater* 1577), Dowr Bud (OC), ?*'dirty river'*

Bude, Estuary (*La Heyle* 1250), Heyl, *'saltings'*

Camel (source to Trecarne) (*Camel* 1284–1748), Dowr Camel, *'crooked one'*

Camel (Trecarne to Estuary) (*Aleyn* 1238–1597), Dowr Alen, (?*meaning*)

Camel, Estuary (*Heyl* 1284, 1722), Heyl, *'saltings'*

Cardinham (*Devyok* 1342), Dowr Devyek, *'cultivated (-land) river'*

Cober (*Coffar* 1283; *Cohor* 1354), Dowr Coghar, *'red one'*

Copperhouse Pool (*Est Lo* 1762), Logh Est, *'eastern inlet'*

De Lank (*Dynlonk* C16), Dowr Dinlonk, *'ravine fort river'*

Dewey (*Duy* 1230; *Duwy* 1241), Duwy, *named for goddess Deua*

Dozmary Pool (ME, *Tosmeri c.* 1300), Tosmery, *'pleasant bowl'*

Durra (*Cendevrion* 977, 1059), Kendevrion, *'waters' meet'*

Durra, Estuary (*Gillyn* 1327, *Kellian* 1507), Kilen, *'creek, inlet'*

Fal (*Fala* 977–c. 1540), Dowr Fala, (?*meaning*)

Fal, Estuary (Tregony to Truro R.) (*Hafaraell* 1049), Havarel, *'fallow-place river'*

Fal, Estuary (Truro R. to sea) (*Careck Rode* 1597), Dowr Carrek, *'rock anchorage'*

Fal, Source (*Penfenton fala* 1320), Penfenten Fala, *'springhead of R. Fal'*

Fowey (*Fawy* 1241–1339), Fowy, *'beeches river'*

Fowey, Estuary (*Uzell c.* 1680), Usel, *'howling place'*

Fowey, Source (*Venton Foath c.* 1680), Fenten Fowy, *'spring of R. Fowey'*

Gannel (*Ganal Creek* 1748), an Ganel, *'the channel'*; (*Willit* 1258, *Gwyllis* 1335), Dowr Gwyles, *'lovage'*

Golitha Falls (*Goletha* C19), Golitha, *'cataract'*

Gunwalloe Stream (*Lofhal, Lovel* 1380), ?Dowr Lovhal, (?*meaning*)

Hayle (*Heyl* 1260–c. 1375), Heyl, *'saltings'*

Helford (*Mahonyer* 1287; *Mawoniek* 1316), Mahonyer, Mawonyek, (?*meaning*)

Kennall (*Keniel* 1296; *Kenel* 1278–1349), Dowr Kenel, (?*meaning*)

Kensey (*Kensi* 1229–c. 1250), Kensy, (?*meaning*)

Kenwyn (*Dower Ithy* n.d.), Dowr Ydhyow, *'ivy trees river'*

Kenwyn, Source (*Venton Wicorriar* 1613), Fenten Wicoryon, *'traders' spring'*

Inny (*Eny c.* 1160–1328), Dowr Eny, *'ash trees river'*

Ladock Water (*Besek* 1547), Dowr Besek, *'finger-shaped'*

Lamorna Stream (*Morno* 1302; *Mornou* 1319), Dowr Mornow, (?*meaning*)

Lamouth Creek, Nans Mogh, *'pigs' valley'*

Lerryn (*Lerion, Leryan* 1289), Dowr Leryon, *'river of floods'*

Loe Pool (*la Loo* 1377; *Lowe* 1501), an Logh, *'pool, inlet'*

Looe (*Loo* 1298; *Lo* 1411), Logh, *'inlet'*

Luney (*Lyveny* 1318), Leveny, *'smooth river'*

Luxulyan (*Werman c.* 1200), Dowr Gwernan, *'alder tree river'*

Lynher (*Lyner c.* 1120–1669), Dowr Lyner, *'lake-like river'*

Lynher, Estuary (*Hallamore* n.d.), Hal an Mor, *'the sea marsh'*

Menalhyl (*Mellynheyl* C19), Dowr Melynheyl, *'mill saltings water'*; (*Glyvion* C12/13), Dowr Glyvyon, (?*meaning*)

Millook Stream (*water of Porthoy* C13), Dowr Porthoy, *'Porthoy river'*

Ottery (*Otery* 1284; OE *otor éa*), Otery, *'otter river'*

Percuil (*Porthcule* 1613), Porth Cul, *'narrow cove'*

Poltesco (*Coger* 1324), Dowr Coger, *'winding stream'*

Red River (Gwithian) (*Dour Coner c.* 1540), Dowr Conar, *'fury river'*

Red River (Marazion to Nancledra) (*Lyd* 1770), Dowr Lyd, (?*meaning*)

Red River (source to Nancledra), Dowr Amal, *'slope/boundary water'*

Ruthern (*Ruthen* 1412; *Rothyn* 1454), Dowr Rudhyn, *'little red river'*

St Allen River, Dowr Alen, (?*meaning*)

St Allen River (source) (*Ventoneage* n.d.), ?Fentenyk, ?*'little spring'*

St Austell (*Winnick* n.d.), Dowr Gwynyk, *'little white river'*; (*Gover* n.d.), Gover, *'stream'*

St Nectan's Kieve (*Nathan's Cave* 1799), Cuva Nathan, *'Nathan's tub'*

St Neot (*Loneny* 1238, *Lonyn* 1241), Lonyny, *'river of small groves'*

Saveock Water (*Dowr Meor* C17), Dowr Meur, *'great river'*

Seaton (*Seythyn* 1302), Dowr Sethyn, *'little arrow river'*

Strat (Neet) (*Neth c.* 1250), Dowr Neth (OC), ?*'clean river'*

Swanpool (*Levine* [for *Lenine*] *Prisklo c.* 1540), Lynyeyn Pryskelow, *'cold pool at Prislow'*

Tamar (*Tamer* 997–1870), Dowr Tamer, ?*'flowing river'*

Tiddy (*Tudi* 1018), Tudy (OC), ?*'people's river'*

Tresillian (*Seugar* 1297; *Sowgar* 1530), Dowr Sowger, (?*meaning*)

Trevillett (*Tredewi water* 1536), Duwy, *'dark river'*

Valency (*Vellinsy, Velinsy* n.d.), Dowr an Velynjy, *'the millhouse river'*

Warleggan (*Mildaldur* 1230; *Bedaldur* 1600), ?Medheldowr, ?*'gentle river'*

Withey Brook (*Withebrook Water* 1613), Withy Brook, *'willow brook'*

Archaeological & historic sites

Antony House (*Castle Anthonie* 1586), Castel Anton, '*Antony Castle*'

Bolster Bank (*Kleth* 1740, *The Gorres c.* 1720), Cleudh '*dyke*'; an Gores, '*the dam*'

Boscawen Un Circle (*Daunce Mine c.* 1680), Dauns Meyn, '*dance of stones*'

Bosigran Castle, Castel Boschygarn, '*castle at Bosigran*'

Boswens Stone (menhir), Men Boswyns, '*stone at Boswens*'

Cadson Bury (OE *Cadoces byrig*), Cadocsbyry, '*Cadoc's fort*'

Caer Bran, Ker Bosvran, '*fort at Brane*'

Caer Kief, Ker Kyf, '*tree-stump fort*'

Caervallack (*Carmailoc* C11/12), Ker Vailek, '*Maeloc's fort*'

Cardinham Castle, Ker Dinan, '*Dinan's fort*'

Carn Euny (*Chapel Uny c.* 1740), Chapel Ewny, '*St Uny's chapel*'

Carne Beacon, Carn, '*cairn*'

Carn Galva Tor Enclosure, (*Castle Anowthan* 1584), Castel an Ohen, '*castle of the oxen*'

Carvossa (*Carwosa* 1480), Ker Wosa, ?'*fort of blood-letting*'

Castle an Dinas (Ludg.) (*Castle Andinas* 1584), Castel an Dinas, '*the hill-fort castle*'

Castle an Dinas (St. Col.) (*Dynas* 1345), Dinas, '*fort*'

Castle Canyke (*Castle Keynok* 1478), Castel Keynek, '*ridge-place castle*'

Castle Dore, Castel Dor, '*earth castle*'

Castle Goff, Castel Gov, '*smith's castle*'

Castle Gotha, Castel Godhow, '*castle of geese*'

Castle Kayle (*Cayl Castelle* 1538), Castel Kel, '*castle of concealment/shelter*'; (*Castel Treclysten* 1478), Castel Treglystyn, '*castle at Treglisson*'

Castle Killibury (*Killiburgh* 1215), Castel Kelly, '*grove castle*'

Castle Pencaire (*Cair Conin c.* 1540), Ker Conan, '*Conan's fort*'

Chapel Jane (*Chapell Innyall* 1580), Chapel Ynnyal, '*chapel at Gurnard's Head*'

Chûn Castle, Castel Chywoon, '*castle at Chun*'

Chûn Quoit, Coyt Chywoon, '*dolmen at Chun*'

Chysauster (*Chysalvestre* 1327), Chysalvester, '*Sylvester's house*'

Dingerein Castle (C18), Din Gerens, '*Gerent's fort*'

Four Burrows (*Bethcywrc* 960), Bedh Crug, '*grave mound*'

Four Parishes Stone (*Meane Crouse* 1613), Men Crows, '*cross stone*'

Geevor Mine (*While an Giver* 1716), Whel an Gever, '*the goats' mine*'

Giant's Castle (Scilly) (*Hengastel* 1305, 1313), Hengastel, '*old castle*'

Giew Mine, Whel an Gew, '*the enclosure mine*'

Helsbury Castle (*Hellesbiri* 1279), Castel Henlys, '*old-ruin castle*'

Hurlers, the (*The Hurlers* 1584), an Hurlyers, '*the hurlers*'

Ince Castle (*Enys* 1427), Castel Enys, '*island castle*'

Lanyon Quoit, Coyt Lynyeyn, '*dolmen at Lanyon*'

Longstone, The (Roche) (*Menevagar* 1660), Men Vagar, (?*meaning*)

Maen Castle (*castle of Meen* C16), Castel Men, '*castle at Mayon*'

Men an Tol, Men an Toll, '*stone of the hole*'

Men Scryfa, Men Scrifa, Men Scrifys, '*stone of writing, written stone*'

Merry Maidens (*Daunce Mine c.* 1670), Dauns Meyn, '*dance of stones*'

Mulfra Quoit, Coyt Molvre, '*dolmen at Mulfra*'

Nine Maidens (Madron) (*Mein yn dans* 1700), Meyn an Dauns '*stones in a dance*'

Nine Maidens (St Col.) (E *Nine Sisters 1584*), Nine Sisters, '*nine sisters*'

Nine Maidens (St Just) (*Meyn an Downze* C18), Meyn an Dauns, '*stones of the dance*'

Nine Maidens (Wendr.) (*Naw-vos c.* 1880), Naw Mowes, '*nine maids*'; (*Naw whoors c.* 1880), Naw Whor, '*nine sisters*'

Nine Maidens (Zenn.) (*Luach an Dygee c.* 1740), Lowarth an Dyjy, '*the cottage garden*'

Pendeen House, Plas Pendin, '*Pendeen mansion*'

Pendeen Vau (*Pendene vowe* 1584), Fow Pendin, '*cave at Pendeen*'

Pendennis Castle, Castel Pendinas, '*castle at Pendennis*'

Pengersick Castle, Castel Pengersek, '*castle at Pengersick*'

Pipers, The (St Buryan) (*The Hurlers* C18), an Hurlyers, '*the hurlers*'

Prideaux Place (*Gwarthendrea* 1702), Gwarth an Dre, '*above the town*'

Restormel Castle, Castel Rostormol, '*castle at Restormel*'

Rumps Cliff Castle (*Pentyre forte* 1584), Din Pentir, '*fort at Pentire*'

St Breock Longstone (*Mene-Gurta* 1613), Men Gortos, '*stone of waiting*'

St Mawes Castle, Castel Lanvausa, '*castle at St Mawes*'

Tintagel Castle (*Durocornovio c.* 700), Din Kernowyon, '*fortress of the Cornovii*'

Tolvan (*Tolvaen* 1302), Tolven, '*hole stone*'

Tregeare Rounds (*Tregaer Castle* 1876), Castel Treger, '*castle at Tregeare*'

Trematon Castle, Castel Tremen, '*castle at Trematon*'

Treryn Dinas (*Castle of Trethyn* 1478), Castel Tredhin, '*castle at Treen*'

Trethevy Quoit (*Trethevy-stones c.* 1605), Meyn Tredhewy, '*stones at Trethevy*'

Trevanson Culverhouse, Colomyer Trevansun, '*dove-cot at Trevanson*'

Wheal Owles, Whel Als, '*cliff mine*'

Wheal Reeth, Whel Rudh, '*red mine*'

Wheal Rose, Whel Ros, '*roughland mine*'

Wheal Vlow, Whel Vlou, '*blue mine*'

Zennor Quoit, Coyt Senar, Coyt Zenar, '*dolmen at Zennor*'

Hills, upland areas, and similar features

Bartinney Hill (*Breteny* 1245), Bre Teny, ?'*rump-like hill*'

Berry Down (*Berydon* 1516; OE *burig* + *dún*), Byrydon, '*fort hill*'

Bin Down (OE, *Béona dún*), Beondon, '*bees' hill*'

Blackendown (*Menadu* n.d.), Meneth Du, '*dark hillside*'

Blacktor Downs (E, *Blaketorrmore* 1401), Black Tor Moor, '*marsh at Black Tor*'

Bodmin Moor (*Goen Bren* C12), Goon Brenn, '*hill downs*'

Brill Hill (*Brehely* 1300), Bre Helhy, '*hunt hill*'

Brown Gelly (*Brongelly* 1283), Bron Gelly, '*grove hill*'

Brown Willy (*Brunwenely c.* 1200), Bron Wennyly, '*swallows' hill*'

Caradon Hill (*Carnedune c.* 1160), Carn, '*tor*'

Carbilly Tor (*Carnebilly* n.d.), ?Carn Ebelly, '*colt's tor*'

Carn, The (Morvah) (*Carnmorvah* 1884), Carn Morvedh, '*Morvah tor*'

Carn Arthen (*Carnarthur* 1454), Carn Arthur, '*Arthur's tor*'

Carn Bean (*Carnvean* 1700), Carn Bian, '*little tor*'; (*Carn Yorth* 1852), Carn Yorgh, '*roebuck's tor*'

Carn Brea, Carn Bre, '*hill tor*'

Carn Eanes (*Carn-inis* 1584), Carn Enys, '*isolated tor*'; (*Carnmele* 1578, *Carn Michael* C17), Carn Mihal, '*Michael's tor*'

Carneglos Tor (Carneglos 1327), Carn Eglos, '*church tor*'

Carn Galva (*Carngalva* 1700), Carn Golva, '*lookout tor*'

Carn Kenidjack (*Carn-usack* 1584), Carn Ujek, '*hooting tor*'

Carnmarth, (*Carne Margh* 1580), Carn Margh, '*horse tor*'

Carnmenellis (*Carnmenelez* 1826), Carn Manalys, '*stacked tor*'

Chapel Carn Brea (*Chapel Carn Bray* 1700), Chapel Carn Bre, '*chapel on a hill cairn*'

Clicker Tor (*monte de Cliker* 1296), Clegar, '*crag*'

Colvannick Tor, Cal Vannek, '*pointed penis (hill)*'

Condolden Beacon (*Gondolvaen* 1298), Goon Dolven, '*hole stone downs*'

Davidstow Moor (*Halmur* 1296), Hal Meur, '*great marsh/moor*'

Dennis Hill (*Dynas* 1356), Dinas, '*fort*'

Dry Carn (*Tricarn c.* 1300), Try Carn, '*three cairns*'

Emblance Downs (OE, *Emlands c.* 1580), Emlands, '*flat-topped lands*'

Garrow Tor (*Garros Moor* 1640), Garow Ros; Gar'ros, '*rugged roughland*'

Godolphin Hill (*Carn Godolcan c.* 1538), Carn Godholcan, '*tor at Godolphin*'

Goon Gumpas, Goon Gompes, '*level downs*'

Goonhilly Downs (*Goenhely* 1300), Goon Helhy, '*hunting downs*'

6

Goss Moor (E, *Gosmour* 1502), Goose Moor, *'goose marsh'*

Hannibal's Carn, Carn Honybal, *'tor belonging to Hannibal (Thomas)'*

Hawk's Tor (*Hokes torr*; OE *hafocas torr*), Hawk's Tor, *'hawk's tor'*

Hayle Kimbro (*Halkimbra* 1841), Hal Kembro, *'Welshman's marsh'*

Helman Tor (E, *Helman Tor* 1696), Helman Tor, *'crag belonging to the Helman family'*

Hendraburnick Downs, Mene'du Hendrebronnek, *'dark hill at Hendraburnick'*

Hensbarrow Beacon (OE, *Hyndes burh*), Hindsburh, *'hind's barrow'*

Hensbarrow Downs (*Goenheyth* 1650), Goon Hedh, *'stag's downs'*

Hingston Down (OE, *Hengesdon* 1297), Hengestdon, *'stallion's hill'*

Kilmar Tor (*Kilmarhe* 1584), Kil Margh, *'horse's back'*

Kit Hill (OE, *cýta hyll*), Kite Hill, *'kite's hill'*

Lanlavery Rock (*Lamlavera* 1440), Lam Lavurya, *'striving leap'*

Louden Hill (OE, *hláw dún*), Lawdon, *'barrow hill'*

Lower Moors (Scilly) (*Gwernewgavell* 1652), Gwernow Gaverhal, *'snipe's alder marsh'*

Men Amber (*Maine Amber* 1584), Men Omborth, *'balanced stone'*

Morvah Carn (*Carnmorvah* 1884; OS, *The Carn*), Carn Morvedh, *'tor at Morvah'*

Mulfra Hill (*Moelvre* 1260–1327), Molvre, *'bare hill'*

Noon Billas, an Woon Bilas, *'the downs of naked oats'*

Notter Tor (OE *hnottan torr*), Nottan Tor, *'bare crag'*

Rough Tor (OE *rúh torr*), Rough Tor, *'rough crag'*

St Agnes Beacon (*Carne Breanick c.* 1720), Carn Breanek, *'tor at Breanick'* (*see* **St Agnes**)

Sharp Tor (OE *scearp torr*), Sharp Tor, *'sharp / pointed crag'*

Sperris Croft (*Croft Speris* 1838), Croft Sperys, *'spirit's rough grazing'*

Stannon Hill (OE *stán dún*), Standon, *'stone hill'*

Tregonning Hill (*Pencair* 1538), Penker, *'fort top'*

Tremollett Down (OE, *Molotedoune* 1337), Molet Down, *'rowel-shaped hill'*

Trencrom Hill (*Torcrobm* 1758), Torr Crobm, *'hunched bulge'*

Trendrine Hill (*Carnminnis* 1700–1813), Carn Munys, *'little tor'*

Watch Croft (*Carnonbigh* 1584), Carnen Bigh, *'little cairn'*

Woon Gumpus (*Nun Compez* 1782), an Woon Gompes, *'the level downs'*

Zennor Hill (*Carn Marrack* 1822), Carn Marhek, *'horseman's tor'*

Coastal features & islands

Aire Point (*Are* 1751), Ardh, '*height*'

Annet (Scilly) (*Anet* 1342–1339), Anet, '*kittiwake*'

Armed Knight (*Guela* C19), Gwela, '*viewpoint*'

Arthur (Scilly) (*Artur* 1500, *Arthures Isle* 1570), Enys Arthur, '*Arthur's island*'

Avarack, The, Havrek, '*summer fallow (ironic name)*'

Bar Point (Scilly) (*Pendrathen* 1652), Penn Drethen, '*end of a sand-bar*'

Barras Nose (E, *Burrows c.* 1840), Barrows Nose, '*promontory with barrows*'

Bass Point (*Beast Point* 1866), Penn Best, '*beast headland*'

Bawden Rocks, Carregy Bodyn, '*rocks off Bawden*'

Berryl's Point (E), Burrell's Point, '*Burrell family's headland*'

Biggal (Scilly), Bugel, '*shepherd, herdsman*'

Bishop Rock (Scilly) (*Maen an Escop* 1302), Men an Epscop, '*the bishop's stone*'

Black Head (St Aust.) (OE, *blæc héafod*), Black Head, '*black head*'; Dyn Garan, Din Garan, '*crane's / heron's fort*'

Black Head (St Kev.) (*Peden due* 1699), Pedn Du, '*black headland*'

Black Rock (Fal.) (*Caregroyne* 1540), Carrek Reun, '*seal rock*'

Blouth Point, Penn Blogh, '*bare headland*'

Brisons,the (F, *Brisant*), Brisant, '*reef*'

Broad Sound (Scilly) (*Haylue Gawen c.* 1588), Heyl Gawen, ?'*Gawen's tidal flats*'

Bryher (Scilly) (*Brayer* 1336), Breyer, '*place of hills*'

Bude Haven (*Beed Haven* 1727), Porth Bud, '*haven at Bude*'

Cadythew Rock (*Carn-due* 1584), Carn Du, '*black crag*'; (*Carrick Due* 1699), Carrek Du, '*black rock*'

Caerthillian Cove (*Gothillan* 1760), Porth Godhelyn, '*stream-bend cove*'

Cambeak, Cambik (OC), '*crooked point*'

Camber Rocks (Scilly), Kemper, '*meeting of currents*'

Camper Porth (Scilly), Porth Kemper, '*cove at a meeting of currents*'

Cannis Rocks (*Canis* 1699), Canys, '*white place*'

Cape Cornwall (*Kilguth East* C17), Kilgoodh Ust, '*goose-back of St Just*'

Caragloose Point, Carrek Loos, '*grey rock*'

Carbis Bay (*Porthreptor* 1580), Porth Reptor, '*cove beside an eminence*'

Carn Aire, Carn Ardh, '*crag on a height*'

Carn Barges, Carn Bargos, '*buzzard's crag*'

Carn Bargus, Carn Bargos, '*buzzard's crag*'

Carn Barra, Carn Bara, '*bread-shaped crag*'

Carn Boel, Carn Bool, '*axe-shaped crag*'

Carn Bras (*Carnvroaz* 1785), Carn Broas, '*great crag*'

Carn Clew, ?Carn Clogh, ?'*bell-shaped crag*'

Carn Creagle, Carn Crigell, *'spider-crab's/cricket's crag'*

Carn Du, Carn Du, *'black crag'*

Carn Gloose (St Just) (*Careg Glouse* 1584), Carrek Loos, *'grey rock'*

Carn Gloose (Zennor), Carrek Loos, *'grey rock'*

Carn Gowla, ?Carn Golva, ?*'lookout crag'*

Carn Greeb, Carn Grib, *'crest/reef crag'*

Carn Gribba (*Carn Greeb* 1862), Carn Grib, *'crest/reef crag'*

Carn Guthensbras (*Guthen Brose* 1751), an Gudhen Broas, *'the hidden reef'*

Carn Haut, Carn Hot, *'hat-shaped crag'*

Carn Ithen (Scilly), ?Carn Edhyn, ?*'birds' crag'*

Carn Kimbra (Scilly), Carn Kembro, *'Welshman's crag'*

Carn Leh (Scilly), Carn Legh, *'slab/ledge crag'*

Carn Leskys, Carn Leskys, *'burnt crag'*

Carn Mahael (Scilly), Carn Mihal, *'Michael's crag'*

Carn Morval (Scilly), Carn Morvil, *'whale's crag'*

Carn Naun Point (*Pensousen* 1582), Penn Sowson, *'Englishmen's head'*

Carn Pednathan (*Cabaneithan* 1866), Capa'n Eythyn, *'the furze cape'*; Pedn Eythyn, *'furze headland'*

Carn Scathe, Carn Scath, *'boat crag'*

Carn Towan, Carn Tewen, *'sand-dune crag'*

Carn Veslan, Carn Vesklen, *'mussel crag'*

Carracks, The, Carregy, *'rocks'*

Carracks, Little (*Carrack an Heythen c.* 1920), Carrek an Edhyn, *'the birds' rock'*

Carrag-a-pilez, Carrek an Bilas, *'rock of the naked oats'*

Carrag Luz, Carrek Loos, *'grey rock'*

Carrick Calys, Carrek Cales, *'hard rock'*

Carrick Gladden, Carrek Gladn, *'waterside crag'*

Carrick Luz, Carrek Loos, *'grey rock'*

Carricknath Point (*Caregnah Point* 1584), Carrek Nath, *'hewn rock'* (*possibly 'puffin rock'*)

Carrickowel Point (*Carrick Owl Rock c.* 1810) Carrek Awel, *'weather rock'*

Carrick Roads (*Careck Rode* 1584), Dowr Carrek, *'rock anchorage'*

Carrickstarne (Scilly), Carrek Starn, *'framework rock'*

Castella (Scilly), Castylly, *'castles'*

Cataclews Point (*carreg loos* n.d.), Carrek Loos, *'grey rock'*

Ceres Rock, Serrys, *'angry one'*

Chair Ladder, Chayr Lader, *'thief's chair'*

Chapel Point (*Goelhofna* n.d.), ?Golowva, *'beacon'*

Chapel Porth (*Porth Chapell* 1699), Porth Chapel, *'chapel cove'*

Church Cove (Gunwall.) (*Porthlingie c.* 1580), Porth Lynjy, *'pool house cove'*

Church Cove (Lizard) (*Lizard Cove* n.d.), Porth an Fos, *'cove of the wall'*

Chynhalls Point, Penn Chy'nals, *'cliff house point'*

Cligga Head (*Clegar* 1588), Clegar, *'crag'*

Clodgie Point (Scilly), Pedn Cla'jy, *'lazar-house headland'*

Clodgy Point (St Ives) (*Cloygva* 1580), Cla'jyva, *'place of a lazar-house'*

Colona Beach (*Caerlaenou* 1329), Porth Kerlenow, *'strip-fields fort cove'*

Constantine Bay (*Egloscontantyne c.* 1525), Porth Egloscostentyn, *'cove at Egloscostentyn'*

Cowloe, ?Cowla, *'curdling'*

Crackington Haven (*Craken Awn* n.d.), Porth Craken, *'cove at Crackington'*

Cragyellis (Scilly) *Trigga Hilles* 1689), Trigva Hellys, *'old ruin of a dwelling'*

Crebawethan (Scilly), Crib an Wedhen, *'reef of the tree'*

Crebinicks (Scilly) (*crebinack* 1744), Cribynek, *'place of small reefs'*

Creeb (Scilly), Crib, *'reef'*

Cribba Head, Penn Cribow, *'head of crests / reefs'*

Crim Rocks (Scilly), Crym, *'pot-sherd'*

Crow Sound (Scilly), Heyl Veur, *'great tidal inlet'*

Cudden Point (*Codan, Coden* 1580), Cudyn, *'curl, tress'*

Daymer Bay (E), Daymark Bay, *'daymark bay'*

Deadman's Cove (*Alsun-Deane Marrame* 1698), Als an Den Marow, *'the dead man's cliff'*

Dennis Head (*Dinas* 1610), Dinas, *'fort'*

Devil's Frying Pan (*Hugga Dridge* 1824), Ogow Dryg, *'low-water cave'*

Dinas Head, Dinas, *'fort'*

Dizzard Point (*Dysert* 1238), Dysert (OC), *'very steep'*

Dodman Point, Penardh, *'prominent headland'*

Dollar Rock, an Dalar, *'the sea-stack'*

Dolor Point, Penn an Dalar, *'the sea-stack headland'*

Downas Cove, Porth Downans, *'deep valley cove'*

Ebal Rocks (*an Eball* 1580), an Ebel, *'the colt'*

Enys, The (Breage) (*Meankeverango c.* 1580), Men Kevrangow, *'hundreds' stone'*

Enys, The (St Just), an Enys, *'the island'*

Enys Dodnan (*Enys Tone* 1580), Enys Dodn, *'turf island'*

Fire Beacon Point (E, *Fire Beacon* 1795), Fire Beacon, *'fire beacon'*

Fistral Bay (E, *Fistal Bay* 1813), Fishtail Bay, *'fish-tail shaped bay'*

Froze Layver (rip-tide, St Just), Fros Lavur, *'labour(ing) current'*

Gaider, The, an Gador, *'the chair'*

Gala Rocks (*Carlow Rocks c.* 1813), Carlyth, *'rayfish'*

Gamas Point, Penn Gammas, *'bay headland'*

Gamper (several), Kemper, *'meeting of currents'*

Ganilly (Scilly) (*Guenelly* 1500), Goon Hyly, *'salt-water downs'*

Ganinick (Scilly) (*Kenenick* 1585), Kenynek, *'place of wild garlic'*

Gazell, an Gasel, *'the armpit (indented cove)'*

Gazick, an Gasek, *'the mare'*

Gell Point (*Cargell Point* 1699), Carn Gell, *'brown crag'*

Gerrans Bay (*Gwyndraith Bay* 1588), Cammas Gwyndreth, *'Gwendra Bay'*

Gew Graze, Kew Gres, *'central hollow'*

Godrevy Island (*the rokket Godrevy c.* 1540), Carrek Godrevy, *'Godrevy rock'*

Gorran Haven (*Portheuste* 1576), Porth Ust, *'St Just's cove'*

Greeb Point (Gorran) (*Greeb* 1732), an Grib, *'the crest / reef'*

Greeb Point (St Anthony) (*The Greeb* 1732), an Grib, *'the crest / reef'*

Greeb Point (Morvah), an Gryb, '*the crest/reef*'

Gribba Point (*Carn Greeb* 1862), Carn Gryb, '*crest/reef crag*'

Gribbin Head (*Penarth c.* 1340), Penardh, '*prominent headland*'

Gribbin, Little (*Grebin* 1699), an Gribyn, '*the little reef/crest*'

Gugh (Scilly) (*Agnes Gue* 1652), Kew Aganas, '*Agnes enclosure*'

Gull Rock (Beeny) (E, *Gulrocke* 1747), Gull Rock, '*gull rock*'

Gull Rock (Portreath) (*Portreyth Island* 1580), Enys Por'treth, '*Portreath island*'

Gull Rock (Trebarwith) (OE, *Otteral* 1748), Oterhal, '*otters' nook*'

Gull Rock (Veryan) (E, *Gray-rock* 1580), Grey Rock, '*grey rock*'

Gulland Rock (*Gullond Rok* 1545), Gullan; Gwylan, '*gull*'

Gullyn Rock, Gullan; Gwylan, '*gull*'

Gunver Head, Gwynvor, '*white sea*'

Gunwalloe Church Cove (*Porth Lingie* C16) Porth Lynjy, '*pool-house cove*'

Gunwalloe Fishing Cove, Porth Wynwalo, '*St Winwalo's cove*'

Gurnard's Head (*Innyall* 1580), Ynnyal, '*desolate*'

Gwavas Lake (*Dowr Gwavas c.* 1680), Dowr Gwavos, '*water at Gwavas*'

Gweal (Scilly) (*Gwithiall Iland* 1652), Gwedhyel, '*place of trees*'

Gwendra Point (*Guyndreth* 1563), Penn Gwyndreth, '*white sand headland*'

Gwennap Head (*Tollpedden Penwith c.* 1670), Tolbedn Penwyth, '*hole headland in Penwith*'

Gwenver, Gwynvor, '*white sea*'

Gwineas or **Gwinges** (*Guin* 1699), Gwyn; Gwynjys, '*white*'; '*windswept*'

Halzephron Cliff (*Alseyeffarn* 1488), Als Yfarn, '*hell cliff*'

Hanjague (Scilly) (*Ingeak* 1655), an Wynjek, '*the windy one*'

Harlyn Bay (*Perleze Bay c.* 1830), Porth Lys; Por' Lys, '*ruin cove*'

Hayle Bay, Porth Heyl, '*cove at the Camel estuary*'

Hellweathers (Scilly) (*Hellveraz* 1655), ?Heyl Viras, ?'*tidal flats to watch for*'

Henscath, Hens Scath, '*slipway*'

Hoe Point (Breage) (*Peden Due* 1794), Pedn Du, '*black/dark headland*'

Holestrow (*Halestrow* C19), Als Trogh, '*broken cliff*'

Holseer, Als Hir, '*long/tall cliff*'

Holywell Bay (*Porraylen* 1688), Porth Heylyn, '*little saltings cove*'

Hor Point, Pen Hordh, '*ram's head*'

Horrace, Hor'es, Hordhes, '*rams*'

Hugo Mesul, Ogow Meskel, '*mussels cave*'

Hyrlas Rock, Hirlas, '*tall, green one*'

Illiswilgig (Scilly) (*Inniswelsick* 1584), Enys Weljek, '*grassy island*'

Innisidgen (Scilly) (*Inezegan* 1584), Enys Ojyon, '*ox island*'

Innisvouls (Scilly), Enys Vols, '*wether island*'

Insworke Point (*Enysworek* C13), Enys, '*island*' (+ OE *geworc*, '*earthworks*')

Isinvrank (Scilly), Enys Vrank, '*Frenchman's island*'

Izzicumpucca (Scilly), Islonk an Bucka, '*the Bucca's chasm*'

Jacka Point (*Jacka* 1866), Choca, Choha, '*jackdaw*'

Jacket Point (E, C16), Jacket's Point, '*Jacket family's headland*'

11

Jangye-ryn, Rynn Yeynjy, *'ice-house promontory'*

Kennack Sands (*Porthkunyk* 1538), Porth Keunck, *'reed-bed cove'*

Kiberick Cove, Porth Keberek, *'timber-strewn cove'*

Killigerran Head, Kil Gerens, *'Gerent's ridge'*

Kittern Rock (Scilly) (OE, *cýta ærn*), Kitern, *'kite's nest'*

Kynance Cove (*Penkynans* 1619), Porth Keynans, *'ravine cove'*

Laden Ceyn (*Lappen Kean, Ladn Keyn* 1876), Labm Keyn, *'leap-back'*

Lamorna Cove (*Port of Nansmorno* 1302), Porth Nansmornow, *'cove of Lamorna'*

Land's End (*Pen an ulays* 1504; *Pedden an wolas c.* 1680), Pedn an Wlas, *'end of the land'*

Lantivet Bay, Porth Nantyvet (OC), *'cove at a cultivated valley'*

Letheggus Rocks (Scilly), Letheges, *'milky ones'*

Lion Rock (*Ennis Vean* 1840), Enys Vian, *'little island'*

Little Hell, Heyl Vian, *'little tidal flats'*

Lizard Point (Cor? E.? F.? *Lesard c.* 1250, 1348), Lesard. ?*'lizard('s tail)'*

Loe Beach (*Loo* 1327), Logh, *'deep-water inlet, ria'*

Logan Rock (*Men Amber* 1870), Men Omborth, *'balanced stone'*

Longships (E, C14), Long Ships, *'long ships'*

Looe Island *see* **St George's Island**

Lucky Hole (E, C19), Lukey's Hole, *'Lukey's hole'*

Lusty Glaze, Lostyn Glas, *'little green tail of land'*

Maen Dower, Men Dowr, *'water stone'*

Maenease Point, Men Ys, *'corn stone'*; (*Penarmeme* 1699), Penn ar Men, *'headland facing a stone'*

Maen-lay Rock, Men Legh, *'ledge stone'*

Maenporth (*Mayne porte* 1584), Menborth, *'stone-cove'*

Maiden Bower (Scilly), ?Men Dowr, *'water stone'*

Manacles, The (*Mannahackles* 1619), ?Meyn Eglos, *'church stones'*

Manare Point, Men Ardh, *'stone on a height'*

Marsland Mouth (OE, *Madocesland múða*), Madocsland Mouth, *'opening at Marsland'*

Mawgan Porth (*Porthglyvyan* 1334), Porth Glyvyan, *'cove of Gluvian'*; (*Porthmaugan* 1755), Porth Maugan, *'cove at St Mawgan'*

Melledgan (Scilly), Men Lehen, *'ledge stone'*

Men a Vaur (Scilly) (*Menavorth* 1689), Men ar Voth, *'stone facing a hump'*

Menawethan (Scilly) (*Mynangwython c.* 1588), Men an Wedhen, *'the tree stone'*

Menbean (Scilly), Men Bian, *'little stone'*

Men-te-heul (*Mean Tale* 1794), Men Tal, *'brow stone'*

Merthen Point (*Merthen* 1732), Merdhin, *'sea-fort'*

Messack Point (*Meysek* 1296), Mesek, *'place of an open field/land'*

Mevagissey Bay (*Porthiley* 1694), Porth Hyly, *'saltwater cove'*

Millook Haven (*Porthoy* 1481), Porth Oy, *'egg cove'*

Minack Point, Meynck, *'stony'*

Minalto (Scilly), Men Altow (OC), *'cliffs stone'*

12

Mincarlo (Scilly), Men Carlyth, '*rayfish stone*'

Morah, The, Morhogh, '*dolphin, porpoise*'

Mother Ivey's Bay (*Polventon Bay c.* 1810), Poll Fenten, '*spring cove*'

Mouls (Scilly), Mols, '*wether*'

Mouls, The, Mols, '*wether*'

Mount's Bay, Cammas an Garrek Los, '*bay of the grey rock*'

Mullion Cove (*Porthmellyn* C18), Porth Melyn, '*mill cove*'

Mullion Island (*Inispriven c.* 1540), Enys Preven, '*worm island*'

Mylor Pool (*Polscatho* 1866), Poll Scathow, '*boats pool*'

Nanjizal Bay (*Nansusel* 1302), Porth Nansusel, ?'*howling valley cove*'

Nare Head (Veryan) (*Penare Point c.* 1540), Penardh, '*prominent headland*'

Nare Point (St Keverne) (*Penare Point* 1540), Penardh, '*prominent headland*'

Nathaga Rocks (*Lethegga* 1838), Lethegow, '*milky ones*'

Navax Point (*Knavocks* 1582), Penn Kynyavos, '*autumn farm headland*'

Newland (*Luland Insula* 1584; *Lueland* 1694), Enys Lulyn, '*fleet pool island*'

Nornour (Scilly), Arnor, '*facing the mainland*'

Northcott Mouth (OE, *norð cot múða*), Northcot Mouth, '*opening at Northcott*'

Northwethel (Scilly) (*Arwothel* 1570), Arwodhel, '*facing watery ground*'

Ogo-dour (*Ugethowr* 1794), Ogow Dhowr, '*water cave*'

Ogo Pons, Ogow Pons, '*bridge cave*'

Old Town Bay (Scilly) (*Porthenor* C12), Porth Enor, '*harbour of St Mary's*'; (*Pereglis* 1708), Porth Eglos, '*church cove*'

Outer Head (Scilly) (*Carnmur* 1655), Carn Meur, '*great crag*'

Padgagarrack Cove, Porth Pajargarrek, '*four rocks cove*'

Park Head (*Pentir c.* 1210), Pentir, '*promontory*'; (*Pencarne Point* C17/18), Penn Carn, '*crag headland*'

Peal Point (*Carreg an Peul c.* 1750), Carrek an Peul, '*the pillar rock*'

Pednavounder, Pedn an Vownder, '*end of the lane/droveway*'

Pednbean (Scilly), Pedn Bian, '*little headland*'

Pedn Boar (*Pedenbore* 1699), Pedn Bor, '*swollen headland*'

Pednbrose (Scilly), Pedn Broas, '*great headland*'

Pedn Crifton, Pedn Cryghton, '*headland with wrinkled turf*'

Pedngwinion, Pedn Gwynan, '*headland at Winnianton*'

Pedn Kei, Pedn Kei, '*dog's headland*'

Pedn-men-du, Pedn Mendu, '*black stone headland*'

Pedn Myin, Pedn Meyn, '*end of stones*'

Pedn Olva, Pedn Wolva, '*lookout headland*'

Pedn Tiere (*Pedntire Rock* 1866), Pedn Tir, '*promontory*'

Pednvadan (*Pentalvan c.* 1540), Pedn Talvann, '*brow-height headland*'

Pelistry Bay (Scilly), (*Porthlistrye* 1650), Porth Lestry, '*haven for ships*'

Pen-a-gader, Penn an Gador, '*the chair (-shaped) headland*'

Penare Point (Mevagissey), Penardh, '*prominent headland*'

Penarrow Point (*Pencarreu point* 1597), Penn Carow, '*stag's headland*'

Penberth Cove (*Porth Penbyrthe* 1580), Porth Benbryhy, '*cove of Penberth*'

Pencabe (*The Cabe* 1732), an Capa, '*the cape*'

Pencarrow Head, Penn Carow, '*stag's head*'

Pendeen Watch, Penn Din, '*fort headland*'

Pendennis Point, Penn Dinas, '*fort headland*'

Pendour Cove, Ben Dowr, '*water's foot*'

Pendower Beach (*Bondowar* 1558), Ben Dowr, '*water's foot*'

Pendower Cove (St Levan) (*Porpendore* 1700), Porth Bendowr, '*water's foot cove*'

Pen Enys Point, Penn Enys, '*island headland*'

Penhale Point (*Penhals-deu* 1600), Penn Alsdu, '*black-cliff head*'

Penhale Sands (*Peran Treth c.* 1600), Peran Treth, '*St Piran's sand*'

Penhallic Point, Penn Helyk, '*willows headland*'

Penhaver Point, Great (*Carlescas Point* 1866), Carn Leskys, '*burnt crag*'

Penhaver Point, Little, Penn Havar, '*headland by summer fallow land*'

Peninnis Head (Scilly) (*Penenis* 1652), Penn Enys, '*end of island*'

Penlee Point (Mousehole), Penn Legh, '*slab headland*'

Penlee Point (Rame), Penn Legh, '*slab headland*'

Pennance Point (*Carne penans* 1590), Carn Pennans, '*crag at Pennance*'

Pen Olver, Pen Olva, '*watchplace headland*'

Penpoll Creek (St Veep) (*Seynt Carroc pyll* n.d.) Pyll Carrok, '*St Carroc's creek*'

Pentewan Beach (*Portbentewen* 1302), Porth Bentewyn, '*cove at Pentewen*'

Pentire Head, Pentir, '*promontory*'

Pentire Point, East (*Pentirbighan c.* 1270), Pentir Bian, '*little promontory*'

Pentire Point, West, Pentir, '*promontory*'

Penveor Point, Penn Veur, '*great headland*'

Penzer Point, Penn Serth, '*steep headland*'

Perbargus Beach, Porth Bargos, '*buzzard's cove*'

Perbargus Point, Penn Porthbargos, '*headland at Perbargus*'

Percuil River (*Porthcule* 1613), Porth Cul, '*narrow cove*'

Perhaver Beach, Porth Havar, '*fallow-land cove*'

Periglis (Scilly), Porth Eglos, '*church cove*'

Pernagie (Scilly), Porth an Ajy, '*cove at the gap*'

Perprean Cove, (*Pordbyghen* 1318) Porth Bian, '*little cove*'

Perran Sands (Perranuthnoe) (*Porth Perane* 1580), Porth Peran, '*St Piran's cove*'

Pibyah Rock, Piber, '*piper*'

Pistol Ogo, Ogow Pistyl, '*waterfall cave*'

Polbream Cove, Poll Breyn, '*filthy cove*' (Next to **Polpeor Cove**.)

Pol Cornick (Gerrans), Poll Kernyk, '*little corner cove*'

Pol Cornic (Mullion) (*Polhorneck* 1841), Poll Hornek, '*iron ore cove*'

Poldhu Cove (*Porthu* 1453), Porth Du, '*dark cove*'

Poldhu Point (*Pedn Poljew* 1876), Pedn Porthdu, '*headland at Poldhu*'

Polgwidden, Poll Gwydn, *'white/fair pool'*

Polhawn Cove, Poll Hawn, *'haven cove'*

Polkirt Beach, Poll Kerhydh, *'heron cove'*

Polpeor Cove (*Polpeer* 1356), Poll Pur, *'clean cove'* (Next to **Polbream Cove**.)

Polpry Cove (*Polprie* 1582), Poll Prei, *'clay pit'*

Polreath (Scilly), Poll Rudh, *'red pool'*

Polridmouth (*Porthredeman* 1443), Porth Redmen (OC), *'stone ford cove'*

Polurrian Cove (*Boloryan* 1580), Porth Beleryon, *'cress-bed cove'*

Polwhevral Creek (*Polwhefrer* 1298), Poll Whevrer, *'lively pool'*

Popplestone Bay (Scilly) (E), Pebble-stone Bay, *'pebble stone bay'*

Pordenack Point (*Poynt Pendenack* 1580), Penn Dinek, *'fortified headland'*

Porn Boe, Porth an Bogh, Por'n Bogh, *'the buck's cove'*

Port Gaverne (*Porcaveran* 1337), Porth Gavryn, (*'cove of the young goat/little cray-fish'* [stream name])

Portgiskey (*Portkiskey* 1760), Porth Kysky, (?*meaning*)

Porthallack, Porth Helyk, *'willows cove'*

Porthallow (*Porthalou* 1290), Porth Alow, *'waterlilies cove'*

Porth Askin (Scilly), Porth Heskyn, *'sedge cove'*

Porthbean, Porth Bian, *'little cove'*

Porthbeor, Porth Buorth, *'cowyard cove'*

Porth-cadjack Cove (*Boscadjack Cove* C18) Porth Boscajek, *'cove at Boscadjack'*; (*Polscatho c.* 1840), Poll Scathow, *'boats pool'*

Porthcew (*Porthcue Cove* 1813), Porth Kew, *'enclosure/paddock cove'*

Porth Chapel (*Porth Sellevan* 1580), Porth Selevan, *'St Selevan's cove'*

Porthcothan (*Porthgohedon c.* 1250), Porth Gohedhen, *'cove by a small barley plot'*

Porth Cressa (Scilly) (*Porthcresse* 1652), Porth Cressa, (?*meaning*)

Porthcurnick, Porth Kernyk, *'little corner cove'*

Porthcurno (*Porth Cornow* 1580), Porth Cornow, *'cove of horns/pinnacles'*

Portheras Cove, Porth Erys, *'plough-land cove'*

Porthglaze (*Porth Loggas* 1580), Porth Logos, *'cove of mice'*

Porthguarnon, Porth Gwernen, *'alder tree cove'*

Porthgwarra (*Porthgorwithou* 1302), Porth Gorwedhow, *'cove by wooded slopes'*

Porthgwidden (Feock), Porth Gwydn, *'white/fair cove'*

Porthgwidden (St Ives), Porth Gwydn, *'white/fair cove'*

Porth Hellick (Scilly), Porth Helyk, *'willows cove'*

Porth Joke (*Porthlejooacke* 1636), Porth Lojowek, *'plant-rich cove'*

Porthkerris (*Porthkersis* 1291), Porth Kersys, *'reed-marsh cove'*

Porth Kidney (*Polkymyas* 1580), Porth Cubmyas, *'cove with permission (to land goods)'*

Porthledden, Porth Ledan, *'broad cove'*

Porth Loe, Porth Logh, *'inlet cove'*

Porthloo (Scilly), Porth Logh, *'inlet cove'*

Porthluney, Porth Leveny, *'cove at the Luney river'*

Porthmellin Head, Penn Porth-melyn, *'headland at Porthmellin'*

Porth Mellon (Scilly), Porth Melyn, *'mill cove'*

Porthmeor Beach (St Ives), Porth Meur, *'great cove'*

Porthmeor Cove (Zennor), Porth Meur, *'great cove'*

Porth Minick (Scilly), Porth Meynek, *'stony cove'*

Porthminster Beach, Porth Mynster, *'endowed church cove'*

Porth Morren (Scilly) (*Porthmoren* 1708), Porth Moren, ?*'berries cove/maiden's cove'*

Porth Nanven (*Porthangwin* 1396), Porth Angwyn, *'Angwin's cove'*

Porth Navas (*Porranavas* 1649), Porth an Navas, (?*meaning*)

Portholland (*Portalan* 1288), Porth Alen, *'cove at the Alen stream'*

Porthoustock (*Portheustek* 1360), Porth Ewstek, *'Eustoc's cove'*

Porthpean (*Porthbyhan* 1297), Porth Bian, *'little cove'*

Porth Saxon (*Porth Zawsen* 1866), Porth Sowson, *'Englishmen's cove'*

Porth Warna (Scilly), Porth Awana, *'St Awana's cove'*

Porthzennor, Porth Senar, Porth Zenar, *'cove at Zennor'*

Port Isaac (*Porthissek c.* 1540), Porth Ysek, *'corn-rich cove'*

Portmellon (*Porthmelyn* 1539), Porth Melyn, *'mill cove'*

Portnadler Bay, ?Porth Nadler, (?*meaning*)

Portquin (*Porthguyn* 1297), Porth Gwynn, *'white/fair cove'*

Praa Sands (*Polwragh* 1331), Poll Wragh, *'hag's/wrasse cove'*

Predannack Head (*Pedn Predanack* 1841), Pedn Predenek, *'British headland'*

Priest Cove (*Porthuste* 1396), Porth Ust, *'St Just's cove'*

Progo, Por' Ogow, *'cavern cove'*

Prussia Cove (*Portlegh* 1345), Porth Legh, *'slab cove'*

Puffin Island (Scilly), (E), Puffin Island, *'island of the Manx Shearwater'*

Queener Point, Penn Keuny, *'reedplace head'*

Quies, The, Gwis, *'sow'*

Rame Head (*Pendenhar c.* 1680), Pen an Hordh, *'the ram's head'*

Rill, The, Ryll, *'cleft'*

Rosen Cliff, Rosyn, *'little promontory'*

Rosemullion Head (*Rosmylyan* 1318), Ros Mylyan, *'Milyan's promontory'*

Rosevean (Scilly), Ros Vian, *'little promontory'*

Rosevear (Scilly), Ros Veur, *'great promontory'*

Round Island (Scilly), an Voth, *'the hump'* (*extrapolated from* **Men a Vaur**)

Rumps, The (*Pentyre forte* 1584), Din Pentir, *'fort at Pentire'*

St Agnes (Scilly) (*Aganas* 1193), Aganas, (?*meaning*)

St Austell Bay (*Trewardreth baye* 1584), Cammas Tywardreth, *'Tywardreath bay'*

St Clement's Isle (*Carn Lodgia* C19), Carn Lojow, *'crag with plants'*

St Columb Porth (*Porbyhan* 1284), Porth Bian, *'little cove'*; (*Por Pennalls* 1699), Porth Penals, *'cove at Penals ('cliff end')'*

St George's Island or **Looe Island** (*Lammana* C13), Enys Lanmanagh, *'monk's church-site island'*

St Helen's (Scilly) (*S. Elid* C12), Elyd, *'St Elidius'*

St Ives Head (*Dynas Ia* 1549), Dinas Ia, *'St Ia's fort'*; (*Pendinas* 1539), Penn Dinas, *'fort headland'*; (*Enys* 1583), Enys, *'island'*

St Loy's Cove, Porth Delow, *'St Delow's cove'*

St Martin's (Scilly) (*Brechiek* 1390), Breghyck, *'many-armed'*

St Mary's (Scilly) (*Enor* 1194–1372), an Nor; Enor, *'the mainland'*

St Michael's Mount, Carrek Loos y'n Coos, *'grey rock in the wood'*

Samson (Scilly) (*S. Sampson c.* 1160–1194), Sampson, *'St Sampson'*

Sennen Cove (*Porth Gonhellye* 1580), Porth Gonhyly, *'harbour for Ganilly'*

Seven Stones (*Lethowsow* 1602), Lethesow, *'milky ones'*

Shark's Fin (St Keverne) (*Carclaze* Rock 1851), Carn Glas, *'green/grey rock'*

Shark's Fin (Sennen) (*Bomear* n.d.), Bogh Meur, *'great buck'*

Sharpnose Point (OE, *scearp næss*), Sharp Ness, *'sharp headland'*

Smith Sound (Scilly) (*Awana Sound* 1652), Dowr Awana, *'St Awana's water'*

Spernic Cove, Porth Spernek, *'thorny cove'*

Stanbury Mouth (OE, *stán byrig múða*), Stonebyry Mouth, *'opening by a stone fort'*

Start Point (*Start* 1841) (OE, *steort*), Stert, *'promontory'*

Steeple Point (OE, *stépel*), Steepel, *'steep place'*

Stepper Point (E, *Stuppert poynte* 1584), Stuppert Point, (*?meaning*)

Strangles, The (OE, *Strangehille* 1391), Stranghyll, *'stream hill'*

Sydney Cove (E), Sydney Cove, (*after Sir Sydney Godolphin C17/18*)

Talland Bay (*Por Tallant* 1699), Porth Tallan, *'Talland cove'*

Tater Du (*Tortell Dewe* 1580), Torthel Du, *'black loaf'*

Tean (Scilly) (*Tyan c.* 1540), Tian, *'St Theona'*

Three Stone Oar (*Euyahore*(?) 1580), Enys Hor', *'ram island'*

Tintagel Head (Cor. or Norman-F? Dyntagel 1302), Dindajel, (*?meaning*)

Toldhu, Toll Du, *'black/dark hole'*

Tolmen Carn (Scilly), Carn Tollmen, *'holed stone crag'*

Tol Pedn Penwith, Tolbedn Penwyth, *'hole headland in Penwith'*

Tol Plous, Toll Plos, *'filthy hole'*

Towan Head, Penn Tewyn, *'sand-dunes headland'*

Trerubies Cove, Porth Treryby, *'Treriby family's cove'*

Treryn Dinas, Castel Tredhin, *'castle at Treen'*

Tresco (Scilly) (*Iniscaw* 1540), Enys Scaw, *'elder trees island'*

Trevelgue Head, Penn Trevelgy, *'headland at Trevelgue'*

Trevone Bay (*Porthmusyn* 1396), Porth Musyn, (*?meaning*)

Trevose Head, Penn Tre'n Vos, *'headland at Trevose'*

Trewavas Head, Penn Trewavos, *'headland at Trewavas'*

Turbot Point (*Gwinyars Head* 1699), Penn Gwynjys, *'headland by Gwineas/ Gwinges rocks'*

Turnaware Point (*Coresturnan* 1323), Cores Tornan, '*weir at a little turning*'

Veryan Bay (*Care Bay* 1646–1715), ?Cammas Ker, ?'*fort bay*'

Vro, The, Brogh, '*badger*'

Wanson Mouth (OE, *wann sand múða*), Wansand Mouth, '*opening by dark sand*'

Watergate Bay (*Tregorrian Cove* 1699), Porth Tregoryan, '*cove at Tregurrian*'

Wheal Edward Zawn (*Porthglaze* C18), Porth Glas, '*blue/green cove*'

White Island (Scilly) (*Nornower* 1652), Arnor, '*facing the mainland*'

Whitesand Bay (*Porthsenan* 1370), Porth Senan, '*cove at Sennen*'

Whitsand Bay (E, *Whitesand Bay* C19), Whitesand Bay, '*bay of white sand*'

Widemouth Bay (OE, *widan múða*), Wide Mouth, '*wide opening*'

Willapark (E, *Willparke* 1556), Well Park, '*well paddock*'

Wolf Rock (E, *The Gulfe* 1564), The Gulf, '*the gulf*'

Yeolmouth (OE, *géol múða*), Yel Mouth, '*opening of a chasm*'

Zawn a Bal, Sawen an Bal, '*the mine chasm*'

Zawn Brinny, Sawen Briny, '*crows' chasm*'

Zawn Bros, Sawen Broas, '*great chasm*'

Zawn Buzz and Gen (*Zawn Posangean* C18), Sawen Bosanjian, '*the giant's dwelling chasm*'

Zawn Carve, Sawen Corf, '*body/corpse chasm*'

Zawn Duel, Sawen Dewal, '*dark chasm*'

Zawn Gamper, Sawen Gemper, '*chasm at a meeting of currents*'

Zawn Kellys, Sawen Kellys, '*hidden chasm*'

Zawn Organ, Sawen Orgel, '*pennyroyal chasm*'

Zawn Peggy, Sawen Pigow, '*chasm by pointed rocks*'

Zawn Polostoc, Sawen Por'lostek, '*fox cove chasm*'

Zawn Pyg, Sawen Pig, '*point(ed) chasm*'

Zawn Reeth (*Sauan Marake* 1580), Sawen Marhek, '*horseman's chasm*'

Zawn Vinoc, Sawen Veynek, '*stony chasm*'

Zawn Wells, Sawen Wels, '*grass chasm*'

Zone Point (*Savenheer* 1597), Sawen Hir, '*long chasm*'

Towns & settlements

Addington (OE, *Eaddan tún*), Addanton, '*Eadda's farm*'

Advent (*Adwyn* 1327), Adwyn, '*St Adwin*'

Albaston (OE, *ánlípigan stán*), Anlipistone, '*solitary stone*'

Allet (*Aled* 1284), Aled, ?'*nourisher (river name)*'

Alsia (*Alsa* 1304–1540), Alsa, '*slope-place*'

Alsia Mill (*Myllynalsey* 1550), Melyn Alsa, '*mill at Alsia*'

Altarnun, Alter Non, '*St Non's altar*'

Amalebra (*Ammalebry* 1302), Amal Ebry, '*lower Amal (river name)*'

Amalveor Amal Vuer, '*great Amal (river name)*'

Amalwhidden (*Ammalwyn* 1334), Amal Wydn, '*white Amal (river name)*'

Anderton (Launcells) (OE, *Onderdune* 1256), Underdon, '*below a hill*'

Anderton (Millbrook) (OE, *Underdon* 1700), Underdon, '*below a hill*'

Anderton (St Juliot) (OE, *Underdon* 1550), Underdon, '*below a hill*'

Angarrack, an Garrak, '*the rock*' (*western Cornish*)

Angarrick, an Garrek, '*the rock*' (*eastern Cornish*)

Angrouse (*Crous* 1317), Crows, '*cross*'

Anhay, an Hay, '*the enclosure*'

Anjarden (*Nansardon* 1692), Nans ar Donn, '*valley facing pastureland*'

Antony (OE, *Anta tún*), Anton, '*Anta's farm*'

Antron (Mabe) (*Anter, Antrenon* C13/14), ?Anter'n Woon, ?'*retreat at the downs*'

Antron (Sithney) (*Antrewon* 1288), ?Anter'n Woon, ?'*retreat at the downs*'

Anvoase (*Voage* 1866), ?an Vos, '*the dwelling/the wall*'

Appledore (E, *Apelderford* 1315), Apelderford, '*apple-tree ford*'

Ardensawah (*Arghansawyth* 1302), Arhansawedh, '*silver stream*'

Ardevora (*Ardevro* 1430), Ardevrow, '*facing waters/rivers*'

Argal, Higher (*Argeldu* 1401), Argel Du, '*black Argel ('retreat')*'

Argal, Lower (*Argelwyn* 1284), Argel Wynn, '*white Argel*'

Argal Manor (*Argel Woen* 1262), Argel Woon, '*Argel at the downs*'

Arrallas (*Arganlis* 1086, *Argansles* 1303), Arhanslys, '*silver court*'

Arrowan (*Arawon c.* 1510), ?Erowan, ?'*acre place*'

Arwenack (*Arwennek* 1285), Arwennek, '*facing the Gwennek stream*'

Ashton (Breage), Ashton, '*ash-tree farm*'

Ashton (Poundstk.) (OE, *æsc tún*), Ashton, '*ash-tree farm*'

Ashton (St Dominick) (OE, *æsc tún*), Ashton, '*ash-tree farm*'

Ashton (St Winnow) (*Aysshe* 1321; OE *æsc*), Ash, '*ash-tree*'

Ayr (*Arthia* 1454), Ardhia, '*St Ia's height*'

Badgall (*Bodgalla c.* 1200), Bodgalla (OC), '*Galla's dwelling*'

Badham (OE, *Badda hám*), Baddham, *Badda's homestead*

Badharlick (*Bodharlek* 1432), Bod Harlek (OC), *'Harlaec's dwelling'*

Bake (Deviock) (OE, *bæc*), Back, *'ridge'*

Bake (Pelynt) (OE, *bæc*), Back, *'ridge'*

Bakesdown (*Baggeston* 1284; OE, **Bæcgas tún*), Baggaston, *'Bæcga's farm'*

Baldhu (Kea), Bal Du, *'black/dark mine-workings'*

Baldhu (Ludgvan), Bal Du, *'black/dark mine-workings'*

Balleswidden, Bal Lyswydn, *'mine workings at Leswidden'*

Balrose (*Balrosa* 1571), Bal Rosow, *'diggings with (water) wheels'*

Balwest, Bal West, *'western mine'*

Bannallack, Banadhlek, *'broom-brake'*

Banns, (St Agnes), an Bans, *'the hollow'*

Banns (St Buryan), an Bans, *'the hollow'*

Barbican (Barvyan 1457), Barvian, *'little summit'*

Barcelona (C17), Barcelona, (*probably named after Catalan city*); (*Trelawne Cross* n.d.), Crowshens Trevelowen, *'crossroads at Trelawne'*

Bareppa (F, *beau repair*), Beaurepair, *'pleasant retreat'*

Bargoes (*Crukbargos* 1424), Crug Bargos, *'buzzard's barrow'*

Barkla Shop (E, C17), Barkla's Shop, *'Barkla family's workshop'*

Barlendew (*Barlendu* 1304), Barlendu, *'summit of a dark strip-field'*

Barncoose, Broncoos, *'wood hill'*

Barnoon, Bar'n Woon, *'top of the downs'*

Barrimaylor (*Merther Melor* 1587), Merther Melor, *'St Melor's grave'*

Barripper (F), Beaurepair, *'pleasant retreat'*

Barteliver (*Baghtylever* 1338), Baghtilyver, *'corner at Tylyver (Lyfr's manor)'*

Bartinney (*Breteny* 1245), Breteny, ?*'rump-like hill'*

Baruppa (F), Beaurepair, *'pleasant retreat'*

Bastreet (OE, *be éastan strǽt*), Byeaststreet, *'east of the road'*

Bathpool (E, C15), Bathpool, *'bathing pool'*

Bawden (*Boden* 1748), Bodyn, *'little dwelling'*

Bawdoe (*Bodou* 1279), Bodow (OC), *'dwellings'*

Beacon (E), Beacon, *'beacon'*

Beagletodn, Begeltodn, *'pasture hillock'*

Bealbury (*Beldebiri* 1317; OE, *Bealdan byrig*), Bealdebyry, *'Bealda's fort'*

Beals Mill (E, C14), Bile's Mill, *'Roger Bile's mill (1338)'*

Bearah (ME, *atte Beare* 1337), Atbeare, *'at the grove'*

Bearland (*Berland* 1284), Berland, *'barley land'*

Bedruthan (*Bodruthyn* 1335), Bodrudhyn (OC), *'Ruthyn's dwelling'*

Bedwindle, Bodwynnel (OC), *'fair-place dwelling'*

Beeny (OE, *byden éa*), Bydeny, *'stream in a hollow'*

Bellowal (*Bollowen* 1309), Bo'lowen, *'happy dwelling'*

Belowda (*Bolowsa* 1503), Bo'lowsa, *'Louda's dwelling'*

Benallack (Grampound) (*Benathelek* 1244), Banadhlek, *'broom-brake'*

Benallack (St Enoder) (*Banathelek* 1302), Banadhlek, *'broom-brake'*

Beneathwood (E, *Bynethewode* 1337), Beneathwood, *'below a wood'*

Benhurden (*Benhordon* 1329), Benhor'dhin, ?'*foot of a ram-fort*'

Bennacott (OE, *Bynnan cot*), Bynnacot, '*Bynna's cottage*'

Benny Mill (E, C16), Bennye's Mill, '*Robert Bennye's mill*'

Bephillick (*Bosfilek* 1319), Bosfylek, '*Fylek's/Felec's dwelling*'

Berepper (F), Beaurepair, '*pleasant retreat*'

Berriow (*Byreyo* 1474; OE, *byrig éa*), Byrya, '*fort river*'

Berriow Bridge (E, C16), Byrya Bridge, '*bridge at Berriow*'

Berry Down (E, *Berydon* 1516), Byry Down, '*fort hill*'

Besore (*Boswoer* 1303), Boswhor, '*sister's dwelling*'

Bessy Beneath, ?Bosveneth, ?'*hillside dwelling*'

Bethanel (*Bithan an hell c.* 1700), Budhyn an Hel, '*the hall's meadow*'

Bethany (Biblical E.), Bethany, '*Bethany chapel*'

Bethel (Biblical E.), Bethel, '*Bethel chapel*'

Bicton (E, *Bucaton* 1337), Bucaton, '*Beocca's farm*'

Bilberry (OE, *Byllan byrig*), Byllbyry, '*Bylla's fort*'

Billacott (*Byllyngcote* 1330; OE, *Byllinga cot*), Byllingcot, '*cottage of Bylla's people*'

Binhamy (OE, *binnan hámme*), Binhamm, '*within the river meadow*'

Binnerton (*Bynner* 1293), Bynner, (?*meaning*)

Biscovey (*Bosconevey* 1201), Bosconevy, '*Cynhaefi's dwelling*'

Biscovillack (*Boscovelec* 1306), Boscovelek, '*Cyfelec's dwelling*'

Bishops Head & Foot (*Meen Crowse an Especk*) Men Crows an Epscop, '*the bishop's cross stone*'

Bissoe (*Besowe* 1327), Besow, '*birch trees*'

Bissom (*Byssam* 1754), Byssam, (?*meaning*)

Blable (*Bleythpol* 1302), Bleydhbol, '*wolf's pool*'

Black Cross, (E, C19), Black Cross, '*black cross*'

Black Rock (E), Black Rock, '*black rock*'

Blackwater (E, C17), Blackwater, '*dark stream*'

Blisland (E? *Glustona* 1086, *Bloiston* 1177), ?Bluston, (?*meaning*)

Blowinghouse (E, C18), Blowing House, '*smelting house*'

Blue Anchor (E), Blue Anchor, (*inn name*)

Blunts (E, *Blunts Shopp* 1687), Blunt's Shop, '*Blunt family's workshop*'

Bocaddon (*Bocadwen* 1507), Bodcadwen, '*Cadwen's dwelling*'

Bochym (*Boschym* 1425), Boschym, (?*meaning*)

Boconnoc (*Boskennec* 1282), Boskenck, '*Cynoc's dwelling*'

Bodardle (*Bodardel* 1284), Bodardel (OC), '*high-stream dwelling*'

Bodargie (*Bodergi* 1315), Bodwurgy (OC), '*Wurci's dwelling*'

Bodbrane (*Bodbran* 1086), Bodbran (OC), '*Bran's/crow's dwelling*'

Bodellick (*Bodelek* 1259), Bo'delek, '*Delec's dwelling*'

Bodelva (*Bodelwyth* 1327), Bodelwyth (OC), '*elm-tree dwelling*'

Boden, Bodyn, '*little dwelling*'

Boderlogan (*Bodelugan* 1324), Bodylogan (OC), '*Ylocan's dwelling*'

Boderwennack, Bo'dreveynek, *'dwelling at Trevennack'*

Bodieve (*Bodyuf* 1323), Bodyuv (OC), *'Yuf's dwelling'*

Bodiggo (*Boswythgi* 1319), Boswydhgy, *'Withgi's dwelling'*

Bodilly (*Bodyly* 1338), Bodyly (OC), *'Ili's dwelling'*

Bodiniel (*Bodynyel* 1284), Bodynyel (OC), *'place of a small dwelling'*

Bodinnar (*Bodener* 1357), Bo'dener, ?*'Dener's dwelling'*

Bodinnick (Fowey) (*Bosdynek* 1396), Bosdinek, *'fortified dwelling'*

Bodinnick (St Stephen) (*Bodythenec* 1281), Bodeythynek (OC), *'furzy dwelling'*

Bodinnick (St Tudy) (*Bodhynek* 1547), Bo'dhynek, *'fortified dwelling'*

Bodmin (*Botmenei* C9, *Bosvena* C18), Bosvenehy, Bosvena *'church-land dwelling'*

Bodrifty (*Bodrythkey* 1344), Bodrythgy (OC), *'Rythgi's dwelling'*

Bodrigan (*Bodrygan* 1284), Bodrygan (OC), *'Rygan's dwelling'*

Bodriviel, Bo'drevyel, *'farm-place dwelling'*

Bodrugan (*Bodrygan* 1329), Bodrygan (OC), *'Rygan's dwelling'*

Boduel (*Botuwel* 1244), Bo'tewal (OC), ?*'dark dwelling'*

Bodulgate (*Bodulgoyd* 1286, 1317), Boduhelgos (OC), *'high-wood dwelling'*

Bodway (*Bodewey* 1302), Bo'dewy, *'Dewi's dwelling'*

Bodwen (Helland) (*Bossewoen* 1302), Boswoon, *'downland dwelling'*

Bodwen (Lanlivery) (*Boswyn* 1296), Boswynn, *'white/fair dwelling'*

Bofarnel (*Bodfernan* 1281), Bodfernan (OC), *'Faernen's dwelling'*

Bofindle (*Bodfelen* c. 1350), Bodfelen (OC), *'Felen's dwelling'*

Bogee (*Bosyuf* 1340), Bosyuv, *'Yuf's dwelling'*

Bohetherick (*Bohydrek* 1402), Bo'hydrek, *'Hidroc's dwelling'*

Bohortha, Buorthow, *'cow-yards'*

Bojea (*Bosyuf* 1340), Bosyuv, *'Yuf's dwelling'*

Bojewyan (*Bosuyan* 1302), Bosuyan, *'Uyan's dwelling'*

Bojewyan Stennack, Stenek Bosuyan, *'tin-stream at Bojewyan'*

Bokenver (*Bodkenver* 1394), Bodkenvor, *'Cynvor's dwelling'*

Bokiddick (*Boskedek* 1278, *Bodcadek* 1284), Boscadek, *'Cadoc's dwelling'*

Boleigh (*Bolegh* 1275), Bo'legh, *'dwelling at a slab'*

Bolenowe (*Boslaynou* 1321), Boslenow, *'dwelling by strip-fields'*

Bolingey (St Mawgan) (*Melyndy* 1216), Melynjy, *'mill-house'*

Bolingey (Perranzabuloe) (*Mellingy* 1516), Melynjy, *'mill-house'*

Bolitho (Crowan) (*Bolleythou* 1278), Bo'leythow, ?*'Leithou's dwelling'*

Bolitho (Menheniot) (*Boleythowe* 1469), Bo'leythow, ?*'Leithou's dwelling'*

Bollowall (*Bolouhal* 1327), Bo'louhal, *'Louhal's dwelling'*

Bologgas or **Bellogas**, Bo'logos, *'dwelling of mice'*

Bolster (*Bothlester* 1398), Bothlester, *'boat(-shaped) hump'*

Bolventor (E, *Boldventure* 1844), Boldventure, *'bold venture'*

Bonallack (*Benathelek* 1321), Banadhlek, '*broom-brake*'

Bone (*Boden* 1327), Bodyn, '*little dwelling*'

Bonyalva (*Pennadeluuan* 1086, *Bannavela* c. 1150) Banadhelva, '*place of broom*'

Bonython (*Bosneythan* 1296), Bosneythan, '*Neythan's dwelling*'

Boquio, Bo'kiogh, '*snipe's dwelling*'

Borah (*Boswragh* 1302), Boswragh, '*hag's dwelling*'

Borgwitha (*Bargwythar* c. 1510), Bargweythor, '*workman's summit*'

Borlase (*Borlas* 1290), Borlas, '*green hummock*'

Borlasevath (*Borlas Margh* 1335), Borlas Margh, '*horse's/Meirch's Borlase*'

Borough (Tresco) (*Cheyncruk* 1314), Chy'n Crug, '*house at the barrow*'

Borthog (*Bosworthogo* 1330), Bosorthogow, '*dwelling at a cave*'

Bosahan (Constantine) (*Bosseghan* 1327–1419), Bossehan, '*waterless dwelling*'

Bosahan (St Anthony in Meneage), Bossehan, '*waterless dwelling*'

Bosanketh (*Bossankuth* 1334), Bosancudh, '*Angawd's dwelling*'

Bosavern (*Bosavarn* 1302), Bosavarn, '*Afaern's dwelling*'

Boscadjack (*Boscadek* 1350, *Boscasek* 1356), Boscajek, '*Cadoc's dwelling*'

Boscarne, Boscarn, '*dwelling by a tor*'

Boscastle (*Castelboterel* 1334), Castel Boterel, '*castle of the Boterel family*'

Boscaswell, (*Boscaswal* 1310), Boscaswal, '*Cadwal's dwelling*'

Boscathnoe (*Bethkednou* 1447), Bedhcadhno, '*Cadnou's grave*'

Boscawen, Bosscawen, '*elder-tree dwelling*'

Boscawen-ros, Ros Bosscawen, '*roughland of Boscawen*'

Boscawen-ûn or **Boscawen Noon**, an Woon Bosscawen, '*the downs of Boscawen*'

Boscean (*Bosseghan* 1302), Bosschan, '*waterless dwelling*'

Boscoppa (*Boscoppe* 1284), Boscoppa, '*Coppe's dwelling*'

Boscrege, Boscrug, '*dwelling by a barrow*'

Boscundle (*Botconwall* 1201), Bosconwal, '*Cynual's dwelling*'

Bosence (St Hilary) (*Boswyns* 1330), Boswyns, '*wind(y) dwelling*'

Bosence (Sancreed) (*Bossens* 1317), Bossens, '*dwelling of holy men*'

Bosfranken, Bosfrynkyon, '*dwelling of Frenchmen/freemen*'

Bosigran (*Boschygarn* 1361), Boschygarn, '*dwelling at Chycarn (lost name)*'

Bosiliack (*Boshouliek* 1303), Boshowlyek, '*sunny dwelling*'

Bosinver (*Bosgenver* 1327), Bosgenvor, '*Cynvor's dwelling*'

Bosistow (*Bosestou* c. 1302), Bosestow, ?'*Estou's dwelling*'

Bosithow (*Bosithiow* 1523), Bosydhyow, '*dwelling of ivy-plants*'

Boskednan (*Boskennen*, *Boskennan* 1303–1597), Boskednen, ?'*Cynan's dwelling*'

Boskenna (*Boskennou* 1321), Boskenow, '*Ceneu's dwelling*'

Boskennal (Ludgvan) (*Boskenhal* 1309), Boskenhal, '*Cynhael's dwelling*'

Boskennal (St Buryan) (*Boskenhal* 1325), Boskenhal, '*Cynhael's dwelling*'

Boskinning (*Boskennen* 1378, *Boskenyn* 1560), Boskenyn, '*dwelling with wild garlic*'

Bosleake, Boslack, '*Laeoc's dwelling*'

Bosloggas (*Boslogos* 1327), Boslogos, '*dwelling of mice*'

Boslow (*Boslowe* 1655), Boslow, '*dwelling where charcoal is made*'

Boslowick (*Bodelewyth* 1301), Boslewyth, '*Leuit's dwelling* '

Boslymon (*Boseloman* 1565), Boseloman, '*Solomon's dwelling*'

Bosmaugan (*Bosmaelgon* 1284), Bosmalgon, '*Maelgon's dwelling*'

Bosoljack (*Bossulsek* 1334), Bossoljek, '*profitable dwelling*'

Bosoughan (*Boshoghan* 1311), Boshoghyn, '*piglet's dwelling*'

Bospebo (*Boospeeby* 1700), Bospiby'/ Bospibyth, '*piper's dwelling*'

Bospolvans (*Bospalven* 1371), Bospeulven, '*dwelling at a pillar-stone*'

Bosporthennis, Bosporthenys, '*dwelling at gateway to Ninnes*'

Bossiney (*Boscyny* 1342), Boskyny, '*Cyni's dwelling*'

Bostrase (St Hilary) (*Bostras c.* 1815), Bosstras, '*dwelling in a flat-bottomed valley*'

Bostraze (St Just) (*Bosstrase* 1732), Bosstras, '*dwelling in a flat-bottomed valley*'

Bosue (*Boshu* 1290, *Boshugh* 1319), Bos Huw, '*Huw's dwelling*'

Bosullow (*Boschiwolou* 1301), Boschywolow, '*dwelling at Chywolow ('house of light')*'

Bosulval (*Boswolvel* 1327), Boswolvel, '*Gwolvela's dwelling*'

Bosvathick (*Boswodek* 1330), Boswodhek, '*stream-place dwelling*'

Bosvenning (*Bosvaenon* 1289), Bosvaynon, '*Maenon's dwelling*'

Bosvigo (*Bosveygou* 1284), Bosveygow, (?*meaning*)

Boswarthan (*Bosvarghan* 1296), Bosvarghan, '*Meirchyon's dwelling*'

Boswarthen (*Bosvarghan* 1338), Bosvarghan, '*Meichyon's dwelling*'

Boswarva (*Bosworweth* 1289), Bosworwedh, '*dwelling at a wooded slope*'

Boswednack (*Boswennek* 1327), Boswednek, '*dwelling by the Wennek stream*'

Boswens (*Boswyns* 1329), Boswyns, '*wind(y) dwelling*'

Boswidjack, Boswijek, '*sow-farm dwelling*'

Boswin, Boswynn, '*white/fair dwelling*'

Boswinger (*Boswingor* 1201, *Boswengar* 1301), Boswengor, '*Uingor's dwelling*'

Bosworgey (St Columb) (*Bosworgy* 1327), Bosworgy, '*Wurci's dwelling*'

Bosworgey (St Erth) (*Boswythgy* 1390), Boswydhgy, '*Gwithci's dwelling*'

Bosworlas (*Bosworlosk* 1284), Bosworlosk, '*dwelling at oft-swaled lan*'

Boswyn, Boswynn, '*white/fair dwelling*'

Botallack, Bo'talck, '*Taloc's dwelling*'

Botathen (*Botadon* 1584), ?Bo'tadhon, ?'*Tadon's dwelling*'

Botrea (*Bostregh* 1314), Bostregh, '*dwelling in a cut-out slope*'

Botternell (*Boturnel* 1244), Bo'dornel, '*Dornel's dwelling*'

Bottoms (E, *Buryan Bottoms* C19), Buryan Bottoms, '*valley bottom at St Buryan*'

Boturnell (*Botornel c.* 1320), Bo'dornel, '*Dornel's dwelling*'

Botus Fleming (*Bodflumiet* 1318), Bodflumyet (OC), '*Flumyet's dwelling*'

Bowda (*Bowode* 1474) (E), Bowood, '*wood where bows are cut*'

Bowgyheere, Bowjyhir, '*long cow-shed*'

Bowithick (*Bodwydok* 1327), Bodwydhek (OC), '*dwelling in a tree-grown place*'

Bowling Green (E, C18), Bowling Green, '*bowling green*'

Box's Shop (E, C18), Box's Shop, '*Box family's workshop*'

Boyton (OE, *Boia tún*), Boyaton, '*Boia's farm*'

Braddock (OE, *brádan ác*), Broadoak, '*broad oak*'

Bradford (OE, *brádan ford*), Broadford, '*wide ford*'

Brane (*Bosvran* 1323), Bosvran, '*Bran's dwelling*'

Bray (*Bre* 1306), Bre, '*hill*'

Bray Shop (E, C17), Bray's Shop, '*Bray family's workshop*'

Brazacott (OE, *Brosyngacote* 1333), Brasingcot, '*cottage of Bras's people*'

Brea, Bre, '*hill*'

Breage (*Eglosbrek* 1181, *Breag* 1602), Eglos Breg, '*St Breaca's church*'

Breja (*Breyssa* 1580), Breussa, '*outermost hill*'

Brendon (*Bremdon* 1296; OE, *brémel dún*), Bremdon, '*bramble hill*'

Breney (*Brenou* 1327), Brennow, '*hills*'

Bridals or **Bridles** (OE, *Brydewille* 1465), Bridewell, '*(St) Bride's well*'

Bridge (*St Julyan's bridge* C16, *Tresulyan* 1699), Resjulyan, '*St Julyan's ford*'

Bridgetown (ME, *Brugge* 1330), Bridge, '*bridge*'

Brighton (E, C19), Brighton, (*?named after Sussex town?*)

Brightor (*Bryghtere* 1326), Bryghtir, '*dappled land*'

Brill (*Brehelgh* 1304), Brehelgh, '*hunt hill*'

Broad Lane (E, C19), Broad Lane, '*wide lane*'

Broadlane (E, C19), Broad Lane, '*wide lane*'

Brockabarrow (E, *Brocka barrow* 1732), Brockbarrow, '*badger's barrow*'

Brocton (OE, *bróc tón*), Brocton, '*stream farm*'

Brooks (E, *Brook c.* 1810), Brook, '*brook*'

Browda (E, *Brodewode* 1330), Broadwood, '*wide wood*'

Brownqueen (*Brangwoyn*, *Bounkoyn* C14), Brongoon, '*downland hill*'

Brunnion (*Bronyon* 1432), Bronyon, '*hills*'

Brynn (*Bren* 1244), Brenn, '*hill*'

Bucklawren (*Boklouvern c.* 1200), Baghlowern, '*fox's corner*'

Buckshead (E), Buckshead, '*buck's hillbrow*'

Bude, Bud, ?'*dirty (river name)*'

Budge's Shop (E, C18), Budge's Shop, '*Budge family's workshop*'

Budock (*Eglos-Budock* n.d.), Eglos Budhek, '*St Budoc's church*'

Budock Vean (*Eglosbuthekbyan* 1469), Eglosbudhek Vian, '*little Budock*'

Budock Water (*Roseglos* 1634), Roseglos, '*church roughland*'

Bugle (E, C19), Bugle, (*after inn built c. 1840*)

Bunning's Park (E, C15), Bunning's Park, '*John Bunnyng's field*'

Burgois (*Borgoys* 1423), Borgoos, '*wood hump*'

Burgotha (*Bargoythou* 1327), Bargodhow, '*top of streams*'

Burlawne (*Bodlowen* 1277), Boslowen, 'happy dwelling'

Burlorne (*Bodlowen* 1277), Boslowen, 'happy dwelling'

Burlorne Eglos, Eglos Boslowen, 'church at Burlorne'

Burlorne Pillow (*Bodlowernpolbrok* 1430), Boslowen Polbrogh, 'badger's pool at Burlorne'

Burncoose (*Broncoys* 1277), Broncoos, 'wood hill'

Burnewhall (*Bodenewel* C10, *Bosdenewel* C14) ?Bos yn Nywl, 'dwelling in mist'

Burngullow (*Bronwolou* 1311), Bronwolow, 'sunlight hill'

Burnthouse (E), Burnthouse, 'burnt house'

Burras (*Berres* 1337), Berres, 'short-ford'

Burraton (Saltash) (OE, *Bureton* 1280), Buraton, 'peasant's farm'

Buryas Bridge (*Nans Berries* 1652), Nans Berres, 'short-ford valley'

Buscaverran (*Boskeveren* 1302), Boskevrang, 'Hundred (border) dwelling'

Bush (OE, *bysca*), Bush, 'thicket'

Bussow (*Bosow* 1284), Bosow, 'dwellings'

Busveal (*Bosvael* 1356), Bosvail, 'Mael's dwelling'

Butteriss Gate, Porth Boderys (OC), 'gate to Boderys (ploughland dwelling)'

Buttsbear Cross (OE, *Bretelesbeorge* 1086), Bretelsbarrow, 'Brythael's barrow'

Cadgwith (*Porthcaswyth* 1542), Porth Cajwydh, 'thicket cove'

Caduscot (*Coldruscot* 1418), Kildreuscuit (OC), 'ridge across a wood'

Caerhayes (*Karihaes* 1259, *Carihays* 1379), ?Caryhays, (?meaning)

Caervallack (*Carmailoc* C11/12), Ker Vailek, 'Maeloc's fort'

Calamansack (*Kilmonsek* 1338), Kilmonsek, 'mounded ridge'

Calenick (*Clunyek* 1334), Clunyek, 'place of meadows'

Callestick (*Kellestek* 1302), ?Kellestek, ?'place of pebbles'

Callington (OE, *Calwetona* 1080), Calweton, 'farm at the bare hill'

Callywith (*Kellegwyth* 1276), Kellywydh, 'grove of trees'

Calstock (OE, *calwe stoc*), Calwestock, 'outlying farm by the bare hill'

Calvadnack (*Calvannek* 1461), Calvadnek, 'prominent point'

Camborne (*Cambron* c. 1100–1816), Cambron, ?'crook-hill'

Cambrose (*Cambres* 1286), Cambrys, 'crook-grove'

Camelford (E, *Camelford* c. 1200), Camelford; Ryscamel, 'ford on the R. Camel'

Camels (*Cammals* 1359), Cammals, 'crooked cliff'

Camerance (*Camweres* 1303), Camweres, 'crooked slope'

Canaglaze (*Caringlaze* 1671), Carn Glas, 'green tor'

Canakey, ?Carn Ky, ?'dog's tor'

Cannalidgey (*Canelysy* 1308), Canelyjy, 'St Idi's channel'

Canonstown (E, C18), Canon's Town, 'canon's farm'

Cant, Canta (OC), 'white/fair place'

Canworthy Water (*Carneworthy* 1327), Carn, 'tor' (+ later OE *worðig*)

Caradon Town (*Carnedune* c. 1160), Carn, 'tor, cairn'

Carbean (*Carnbyan* 1356), Carn Bian, 'little tor'

Carbis (Roche) (*Carbons* 1303), Carbons, *'paved way'*

Carbis Bay (cove) (*Porthreptor* 1580), Porth Reptor, *'cove beside an eminence'*

Carbis Bay (village) (*Carbons* 1391), Carbons, *'paved way'*

Carbis Mill (St Hilary) (*Carbows* 1564), Carbons, *'paved way'*; (*Rosmelin* 1233), Rosmelyn, *'mill roughland'*

Carburrow (*Carbura* 1256), Ker Bora, *'boar's fort'*

Carclaze (*Cruklas c.* 1500), Crug Las, *'green barrow'*

Carclew (*Crukleu* 1327), Crug Lyw, *'barrow of colour'*

Cardew (Trevalga) (*Cartheu* 1327), Ker Dhu, *'black/dark fort'*

Cardew (Warbstow) (*Carthu* 1334), Ker Dhu, *'black/dark fort'*

Cardinham (*Cardynan* 1284), Ker Dinan, *'fort (tautol.)'*

Cardrew (*Caerdro* 1311, *Caerdreu* 1356), Ker Dro, *'fort at a turning'*

Carevick (*Crowarthevycke* 1567), Crow war Dhyvyk, *'Crow ('hut') on unusable land'*

Carfury (*Carnfuru* 1327), Carn Furow, *'wise men's tor'*

Cargelley (*Cargelly* 1332), Ker Gelly, *'grove fort'*

Cargentle (*Cargyntell* 1287), Ker Guntell, *'assembly fort'*

Cargenwen (*Cargenwyn* 1375), Ker Genwyn, *'Cenwyn's fort'*

Carglonnan (*Kylglynan* 1327), Kilglynen, *'ridge by a small deep valley'*

Cargloth (*Cargluthan* 1432), Ker Gleudhyn *'fort by a small ditch'*

Cargoll (*Cargaul* 1302), Ker Gowl, *'fort at a fork'*

Cargreen (*Carrecron* 1018), Carrek Reun, *'seal rock'*

Carharrack (*Cararthek* 1250), Ker Ardhek, *'Arthoc's fort'*

Carhart (*Kaerhorta c.* 1250), Ker Hordha, *'ram-place fort'*

Carines (*Crowarthenys* 1398), Croworthenys, *'hut by detached land'*

Carkeel (*Karkil* 1280), Ker Kil, *'ridge fort'*

Carland Cross (E, *Cowland* 1813), Cowland, *'cow land'*

Carleen (Breage) (*Carleghyon* 1262), Ker Leghyon, *'slabs fort'*

Carleen (Mawgan) (*Carleyn* 1548), Ker Len, *'strip-field fort'*

Carleon (*Carleghion* 1339), Ker Leghyon, *'slabs fort'*

Carlidnack (*Carlunyek* 1333), Ker Lunyek, (*?meaning*)

Caerloggas (St Columb) (*Kaerlogoos c.* 1320), Ker Logos, *'fort of mice'*

Carloggas (St Mawgan) (*Cruclogas* 1284), Crug Logos, *'barrow of mice'*

Carloggas (St Stephen) *Cruglogos* 1282), Crug Logos, *'barrow of mice'*

Carluddon (*Crucledan* 1364), Crug Ledan, *'wide barrow'*

Carlyon (*Carleghion* 1287), Ker Leghyon, *'slabs fort'*

Carlyon Bay (Higher Polmer 1794), Porthmeur Wartha, *'higher Polmear (great cove)'*

Carminow Cross (*Kayrminow c.* 1240), Ker Menow, *'fort of stones'*

Carn, Carn, *'tor'*

Carnanton (*Carnanton* 1303), Carnen, *'cairn'*

Carn Arthen (*Carnarthur* 1454), Carn Arthur, *'Arthur's tor'*

27

Carn Brea, Carn Bre, *'hill tor'*

Carn Towan, Carn Tewyn, *'sand-dunes crag'*

Carnclaze, Carn Glas, *'green/grey tor'*

Carne (Lanteglos by Fowey) (*Talcarne* 1370), Talcarn, *'brow tor'*

Carne (St Dennis), Carn, *'tor'*

Carne (St Keverne), Carn, *'tor'*

Carne (Veryan), Carn, *'cairn'*

Carne, South (Altarnun) (*Suth Carn* 1314), Carn Soth, *'south Carne'*

Carne, West (Altarnun), (*Westcarn* 1350), Carn West, *'west Carne'*

Carnebone (*Carnebwen* 1298), Carn Ebwyn, *'Ebwyn's tor'*

Carnelloe, Carnellow, *'little crags'*

Carnequidden (*Kernekwyn* 1367), Kernykwydn, *'white corner'*

Carnevas (*Crucneves* c. 1250), Crug Neves, *'barrow at a sacred grove'*

Carnewas (*Carneues* 1306, *Canhewas* 1748), Carn Havos, *'crag at a shieling/summer grazing'*

Carnhell Green (*Carnhel* 1302), Carn Hel, *'hall tor'*

Carnhot, Carn Hot, *'hat-shaped tor/cairn'*

Carnkie (Redruth) (*Carnkye* 1720), Carn Kei, *'dog tor'*

Carnkie (Wendron) (*Carnky* 1298), Carn Kei, *'dog tor'*

Carnkief (*Carnkef* C13), Carn Kyf, *'tree-stump tor'*

Carnmeal (*Carnmele* 1501), Carn Mel, *'honey tor'*

Carnmenellis (*Carnmenelez* 1826), Carn Manalys, *'stacked tor'*

Carnon Downs (*Goon Carnon* 1782), Goon Carnen, *'little cairn downs'*

Carnpessack, Carn Pesek, *'decayed crag'*

Carnsew (Hayle) (*Carndu* 1298), Carn Du, *'black crag'*

Carnsew (Mabe) (*Carnduwyou* 1309), Carn Duwyow, *'gods' tor'*

Carnsmerry (*Carna Rosemerry* 1660), Carn Rosmeur, *'great roughland tor'*

Carnyorth (*Carnyorgh* 1334), Carn Yorgh, *'roebuck tor'*

Caroe (*Cayrou* 1327), Kerrow, *'forts'*

Carpalla (*Carnpalla* 1336), ?Carn Pella, ?*'further tor'*

Carracawn (*Caricon* 1291), Carrek On, *'lamb's/ash-trees rock'*

Carrancarrow (*Nankerou* 1366), Nanscarow, *'stag's valley'*

Carrine (*Caryeyn* 1280), Ker Yeyn, *'cold fort'*

Carruggatt (*Carhulgat* c. 1170), Ker Uhelguit (OC), *'high-wood fort'*

Carsawsen, Ker Sowson, *'Englishmen's fort'*

Carthew (St Austell), Ker Dhu, *'black/dark fort'*

Carthew (Wendron), Ker Dhu, *'black/dark fort'*

Cartole (*Cruktoll* 1284), Crug Toll, *'hole/hollow barrow'*

Cartuther (*Cructuther* 1328), Crug Teudar, *'Teudar's barrow'*

Carvannel (*Kaervanathel* 1302), Ker Vanadhel, *'broom fort'*

Carvedras (*Carvodret* c. 1250), Ker Vodres, *'Modret's fort'*

Carveth (*Carvergh* 1538), Ker Vergh, *'horses' fort'*

Carvinack (Penryn) (*Kerwynnec* 1288), Ker Wynnek, *'fort by the Gwynnek stream'*

Carvinack (St Enoder) (*Carvynek* 1547), Ker Veynek, '*stony fort*'

Carvinack (St Just in Roseland) (*Carveynek* C14) Ker Veynek, '*stony fort*'

Carvinick (Goran) (*Carveynek* 1333), Ker Veynek, '*stony fort*'

Carvolth (*Carvolgh c.* 1400), Ker Volgh, '*gap fort*'

Carvossa (*Carwosa* 1480), Ker Wosa, ?'*fort of blood-letting*'

Carwarthen (*Carwenran* 1314), Ker Wenran, '*Uuenran's fort*'

Carwen (*Carwen* 1327), Ker Wenn, '*white/fair fort*' (*fem. of* **gwynn**)

Carwinion (*Caerwengeyn* 1334), Ker Wengeyn, '*white-ridge fort*'

Carwithan (*Caerwitha* 1284), Ker Witha, '*guarding fort*'

Carwynnen, Ker Wynen, (?*meaning*)

Carwythenack (*Kayrwethenec* 1303), Ker Wedhenek '*Guethenoc's fort*'

Carzise (*Kaerseys* 1281), Ker Seys, '*Englishman's fort*'

Castallack (*Castellek c.* 1540), Castellek, '*fortified*'

Castilly, Castylly, '*castles*'

Castle Dewey (*Castelduy* 1327), Castelduwy, '*castle on the river Dewey*'

Castle Gate (E, C19), Castle Gate, '*castle gate*'

Castle Horneck (*Castelhornek* 1335), Castel Hornek, '*iron-like castle*'

Castlewich (*Castlewyk* 1284), Castelwyk, '*castle at a forest settlement*'

Castlezens, Castelsens, '*holy men's castle*'

Catchall (inn name: *Lr. Hendra* 1840), Hendre Woles, '*lower Hendra (home farm)*'

Catchfrench (F, *Cachefranshe* 1458), Chasefranch, '*free chase/hunting ground*'

Cathebedron (*Caderbaderen* 1286), Cadorbedren, '*chair for the backside*'

Cawsand (E, *Couyssond* 1405), Cowssand, '*cow's sand*'

Chacewater (E, C17), Chasewater, '*stream on hunting ground*'

Chapel (St Col. Mnr.) (*Chapelkernewyl* 1302), Chapel Kernwhily, '*lapwings chapel*'

Chapel Amble (*Amaleglos* 1284), Amal Eglos, '*church on R. Amble ('boundary')*'

Charaton (OE, *ceorles tún*), Churlston, '*freeman peasants' farm*'

Charlestown (*Portmoer* 1354), Porth Meur, '*great cove*'

Cheesewarne (*Chisorne* 1588), Chysorn, '*house at a nook*'

Chegwidden (Constantine) (*Chygwen* 1304), Chy Gwydn, '*white house*'

Chegwins, Chy Gwyns, '*wind(y) house*'

Chegwyne (Kea) (*Chigwin* 1634), Chy Gwynn, '*white house*'

Chenhalls (*Chynals* 1453), Chy'n Als, '*house at the cliff*'

Chilsworthy (OE, *Ceoles worðig*), Chilsworthy, '*Ceol's holding*'

Chirwyn, Chy Run, '*house on a slope*'

Chiverton (Perranuthnoe) (*Chiwarton* 1311), Chy war Tonn, '*house on pastureland*'

Chiverton (Sancreed) (*Chwyarton* 1338), Chy war Tonn, '*house on pastureland*'

Chiverton (Silverwell), Chy war Tonn, '*house on pastureland*'

Cholwell (E, *Choldewylle* 1428), Coldwell, '*cold well/stream*'

Chûn (*Cheiwone* 1283, *Chywone* 1508), Chy Woon, '*downs house*'

Church Combe (E), Church Cumb, *'church valley'*

Church Cove (Gunwalloe) (*Porthlingie c.* 1580), Porth Lynjy, *'pool house cove'*

Church Cove (Landewednack) (*Perran Vose* 1851), Porth an Fos, *'cove of the wall'*

Chyandour, Chy an Dowr, *'house at the stream'*

Chyangweal, Chy an Gwel, *'house at the open field'*

Chyanvounder, Chy an Vownder, *'house at the lane'*

Chybucca (*Guenbuck* 1714, *Woon Bucka c.* 1790) Woon Bucka *'goblin's/scarecrow's downs'*

Chycoose (*Chiencoys* 1378), Chy an Coos, Chy'n Coos, *'house at the wood'*

Chycowling (*Chycowlyng* 1554), Chy Cowlyng, *'Cowlyng family's house'*

Chyenhal, Chy an Hal, *'house at the marsh'*

Chykembro, Chy Kembro, *'Welshman's house'*

Chynhale (Perranzab.) (*Chyenhale* 1356), Chy an Hal, Chy'n Hal, *'house at the marsh'*

Chynhalls, Chy an Als, Chy'n Als, *'house at the cliff'*

Chynoweth, Chy Nowyth, *'new house'*

Chyoone (Paul) (*Chyunwone* 1274), Chy an Woon, *'house on the downs'*

Chypons, Chy Pons, *'bridge house'*

Chypraze, Chy Pras, *'meadow house'*

Chyreen (*Chywarrin* 1419), Chy war Rynn, *'house on a slope'*

Chysauster (*Chisalvestre* 1313), Chy Salvester, *'Sylvester's house'*

Chytane (*Tywarton* 1296, *Chyton* 1543), Chy war Tonn, *'house on pastureland'*

Chytodden (Camborne) (*Chywarton* 1538), Chy war Todn, *'house on pastureland'*

Chytodden (Towednack) (*Chyenton* 1320), Chy an Todn, *'house at the pastureland'*

Chyvarloe (*Chywarlo* 1300), Chy war Logh, *'house on an inlet'*

Chyvelah (*Chywela* 1836), Chy Whila, *'beetle-infested house'*

Chyvellan, Chy Velyn, *'mill-house'*

Chyvogue (*Chifoage* 1634), Chy Vog, *'furnace house'*

Chywoon (Germoe) (*Chywone* 1531), Chy Woon, *'downs house'*

Chywoone (Breage) (*Cheienwoen* 1329), Chy an Woon, *'house on the downs'*

Chywoone (St Keverne) (*Chyenwoen* 1300), Chy an Woon, *'house on the downs'*

Clampit (OE, *clám pytt*), Clampit, *'muddy hollow, claypit'*

Clann (*Kellilan* 1309), Kellylan, *'grove at a church enclosure'*

Clapper Mill, Melyn Clappya, *'chattering mill'*

Cleave (*Cliffe* 1480; OE, *clif*), Cliff, *'cliff, slope'*

Cleers (*Cleher* 1516), Cleher, (?*meaning*)

Cleese (*Cleys* 1420), Cleys, *'ditch'*

Clennick (*Clunyok* 1284), Clunyek, *'meadow place'*

Clerkenwater (OE, *clercen wæter*), Clerkenwater, *'student's stream'*

Cliff (OE, *clif*), Cliff, *'steep hillside, river bank'*

Clijah, Cleyjow, *'ditches'*

Clowance (*Clewyns* 1362), Clewyns, ?*'hear-wind'*

Clowne, Clun, *'meadow'*

Clubworthy (*Clobiry* 1322) (OE, **clóh byrig*), Clobyry, ?'*ravine fort*'

Coad's Green (E, C18), Coade's Green, '*Coade family's green*'

Cocks (E, C18), Cookes, '*Cooke family's holding*'

Cockwells (E, C17), Cockwells, '*Cockwell family's holding*'

Codda (*Stumcodda* 1280), Stumcodda, '*Codde's bend*'

Cojegoes (*Cozejegowe* C17), Coos Heyjygow, '*ducklings' wood*'

Colan (*Plewe-Golen* 1501), Pluw Golan, '*St Colan's parish*'

Cold Northcott (OE, *Northcott* 1608), Northcot, '*northern cottage*'

Coldharbour (St Agnes) (*Gyllyveor c.* 1600), Kelly Veur, '*great Kelly (grove)*'

Coldrenick (*Kyldreynak* 1302), Kildreynek, '*thorny nook*'

Coldrinnick (*Kyldreynak* 1302), Kildreynek, '*thorny nook*'

Coldvreath (*Kellyvregh* 1281), Kelly Vregh, '*dappled grove*'

Colenso (*Kelensou* 1334, *Kelensowe* 1406), Kelynsow, (?*meaning*)

Colesloggett (*Castle Loggett* 1733), Castel Logot (OC), '*castle of mice*'

Colgrease (*Crowgres* 1498), Crowgres, '*middle Crow ('hut')*'

Collamoor Head (OE, *Collamore* 1613), Collamoor, '*Colla's marsh*'

Colliford (E, *Colaford* C13), Colaford, '*Cola's ford*'

Colloggett, Killogot (OC), '*ridge of mice*'

Collurian (probably Gk), Colorion, '*eye-salve*'

Colona (*Caerlaenou* 1329), Ker Lenow, '*fort by strip fields*'

Colquite (*Kilcoit* 1175), Kilcuit (OC), '*wood ridge*'

Colvannick (*Calvannek* 1327), Calvannek, '*pointed penis (hill)*'

Colvithick (*Kelwethek* 1302, *Colvethicke* 1613), Collwedhek, '*place of hazel trees*'

Come-to-good (E, C18), Come to God, '*come to God*'

Comford (*Coumfort* 1768), Comfordh, '*valley road*'

Comfort (*Comforth* 1609), Comfordh, '*valley road*'

Commonmoor (E, C19), Common Moor, '*marsh of common grazing*'

Comprigney (*Gwele Cloke-prynnyer* 1597), Gwel Cloghprennyer, '*gallows field*'

Conce (*Cawnce* 1613), Cons, Cauns, '*paved road*'

Condurrow (*Kendorou* 1327), Kendowrow, '*meeting of streams*'

Congdon's Shop (E, C18), Congdon's Shop, '*Congdon family's workshop*'

Connerton (*Connartona* 1147), Conar, '*fury (river name)*' (+ OE *tún*)

Connon Bridge (E, *Convent c.* 1290), Convent Bridge, '*convent bridge*'

Connor Downs (*Conner Down* 1813), Goon Conar, '*downs at Conerton*'

Constantine (*Langostentin* 1574), Langostentyn, '*St Constantine's church-site*'

Constantine Bay (*Egloscontantyne c.* 1525), Eglos Costentyn, '*St Constantine's church*'

Cooksland (E, C16), Cooke's Land, '*Cooke family's holding*'

Coombe (Camborne), Comm, '*valley*'

Coombe (Gwennap) (E, C19), Comm, '*valley*'

Coombe (Kea), Comm, '*valley*'

Coombe (St Stephen), Comm, '*valley*'

Coombe (Morwenstow), Comm, *'valley'*

Coombe (Dobwalls), Comm, *'valley'*

Coosebean (*Cusbyan c.* 1400), Coosbian, *'little wood'*

Coosewartha (*Coozwarra* 1748), Cooswartha, *'higher wood'*

Coppathorne (OE, *coppe þorn*), Copthorn, *'pollarded thorn tree'*

Copperhouse (E, C19), Copperhouse, *'copper smelting house'*

Copthorne (OE, *coppe þorn*), Copthorn, *'pollarded thorn tree'*

Corgee (*Corngae* 1279), Cornge, *'corner of a hedge'*

Corgerrick (*Kugurryk* 1342), Cogeryk, *'little Kuggar'*

Cornakee (OE, *cornuc éa*), Cornaky, *'crane's stream'*

Corneal (*Cornhele* 1305; OE, *corna healh*, Cornhal, *'crane's corner'*

Cornelly, Cornely, *'St Cornelius'*

Cosawes (*Cosawyth* 1284), Cosawedh, *'stream wood'*

Costislost (E, C19), Costislost, *'unprofitable land'*

Coswarth (OE, *Cudiford* 1340), Codaford, *'Coda's ford'*

Coswinsawsin, Coswynn Sowson, *'white/fair wood of the English'*

Cotehele (*Cotheyle* 1302), Cuitheyl (OC), *'wood by tidal flats'*

Cotna (*Cruckonnar* 1289), Crug Conar, *'Conar's barrow'*

Couch's Mill (E, C14), Melyn Cogh, *'Couch family's mill'*

Coverack (*Porthkoverec* 1284), Porth Coverek, (?*meaning*)

Coverack Bridges (*Cofrek* n.d.), Pons Cogharyk, *'bridge on the little Cober'*

Cowlands (*Cownance* 1631), Cownans, *'deep/enclosed valley'*

Cow-y-jack (*Kewedyk* 1312), Kewejek, Cowejek, *'hollowed'*

Cox Hill (E), Cox's Hill, *'Cox family's hill'*

Coxford (E, *Cokkysford* 1414), Coksford, *'Cok family's ford'*

Coxpark (E, *Cox's Park* 1884), Cox's Park, *'Cox family's parkland'*

Crackington (*Crakenton* 1181), Craken, *'little crag'*

Crackington Haven, Porth Craken, *'cove at Crackington'*

Crafthole (OE, *croft holh*), Crofthole, *'hollow with enclosed arable land'*

Crahan (*Caraghen* 1370), Ker Ahen, *'henbane fort'*

Crane (*Caervran c.* 1260), Ker Vran, *'crow's/Bran's fort'*

Crankan (Heamoor) (*Trevrankan* 1327), Trevrankyon, *'freemen's farm'*

Crankan (Madron) (*Caranken* 1346), Ker Anken, *'fort of misery'*

Crantock (*Langorroc* 1086), Langorrek, *'Goroc's church-site'*

Creak-a-vose (*Crucgkeyrvos* 1346), Crug Kervos, *'barrow at a fort rampart'*

Crean (*Kacregan* 1238), Kecrugyn, *'hedge by a small barrow'*

Creed, Crid, *'St Crida'*

Creegbrawse, Crug Broas, *'large barrow'*

Cregoe (*Crugou* 1284), Crugow, *'barrows'*

Crelly (*Caryly* 1284), Ker Yly, *'Yli's fort'*

Cremyll (OE, *crymel*), Crymel, *'fragment of land'*

Crenver (*Caergenver* 1201), Ker Genvor, *'Cynvor's fort'*

Criffle (*Cryffyl* 1451), Cryghel, *'wrinkled place'*

Crift (*Croft* 1609), Croft, *'enclosed rough grazing'*

Criggan (*Crugan* 1533), Crugyn, *'small barrow'*

Crinnis (*Caryones* 1477), Caryones, (*?meaning*)

Crimp (OE, *crumpe*), Crump, *'crooked'*

Cripples Ease (E, C19), Cripples' Ease, (*ironic name for a hilltop inn*)

Croanford (*Crowen* 1302), Crowyn, *'small hut'*

Crockett (*Knoket* 1348), Kneghcuit (OC), *'knoll wood'*

Croft Mitchell, Croft Mihal, *'Michael's rough grazing land'*

Crofthandy (*Croft Hendy* 1794), Croft Hendy, *'rough grazing by a ruined house'*

Croft Michell or **Michael**, Croft Mihal, *'Michael's enclosed rough grazing'*

Croft Pascoe (C17), Croft Pasco, *'Richard Paskoe's rough grazing'*

Cross Coombe, Comcrows, *'valley with a cross'*

Cross Hill (E), Cross Hill, *'hill with a cross'*

Cross Lanes (Cury) (E, C19), Cross Lanes, *'junction of lanes'*

Crossgate (E), Cross Gate, *'gate by a cross'*

Crousa (*Crouswrach* 977), Crowswragh, *'hag's cross'*

Crows Nest (E, C17), Crow's Nest, *'high place'*

Crowan (*Egloscraweyn* 1580), Eglos Crewen, *'St Crewen's church'*

Crowdy, Crowdy (OC), *'hut'*

Crowgey, Crowjy, *'hut'*

Crowlas (*Creures* 1327), Crewres, *'weir/stepping stones ford'*

Crowntown (E), Crowntown, *'settlement at the Crown Inn'*

Crows-an-wra (*Crouzenwragh* 1732), Crows an Wragh, *'the hag's cross'*

Crowsmeneggus (*Rosemenewas* 1660), Rosmenawes, *'awl-shaped hillspur'*

Crugmeer (*Crucmur* 1339), Crug Meur, *'large barrow'*

Crugsillick (*Crugsulek* 1302), Crug Sulek, *'Suloc's barrow'*

Crumplehorn (*Tremylhorne* 1565), Tremalhorn, *'Maelhoern's farm'*

Cubert (*Egloscubert* 1622), Eglos Cubert, *'St Cubert's church'*; (*Lanowyn* 1622), Lanoweyn, *'Owein's church enclosure'*

Cuby, Kyby, *'St Kybi'*

Cuddenbeak (*Cotynbeke* 1330), Cuitynbyk (OC), *'little point-wood'*

Cuddra (*Crukdur* 1299), Crug Dowr, *'stream barrow'*

Culdrose, Culros, *'narrow roughland'*

Curgurrel (*Crugeler* 1314), Crug Geler, *'coffin barrow'*

Currian Vale (*Venton Currian* 1695), Fenten Goryon, *'hosts'/clans' spring'*

Curry, East (*Cory* C14), Cory Est, (*?meaning*)

Curry, West, Cory West, (*?meaning*)

Cury (*Egloscuri* 1219), Eglos Cury, *'St Cury's (Corantyn's) church'*

Cusgarne (*Coysgaran* 1277), Cosgaran, *'crane's/heron's wood'*

Cusveorth, Cosvuorth, *'cow-yard wood'*

Cutbrawn (*Cutbrayn* 1476), Cuitbran (OC), *'crow's/Bran's wood'*

Cutcare (*Cutkayrowe* 1600), Cuitkerrow (OC), *'forts wood'*

Cutkieve, Cuitkyf, '*stump wood*'

Cutmadoc (*Coysmadoc* 1314), Cosmadek (part OC), '*Madoc's wood*'

Cutmere, Cuitmeur (OC), '*large wood*'

Cutparrett (*Cut Pervet* 1324), Cuitpervet (OC), '*middle/inner wood*'

Dannett (*Dounant* 1303), Downant (OC), '*deep valley*'

Darite (*Daryet* 1506; OE, *déor geat*), Deergate, '*deer gate*'

Darley (*Durklegh* 1296; OE, *deorc léah*), Darklea, '*dark clearing*'

Davidstow (*S. David* 1269, *Dewystowe* 1395), Dewy, '*St Dewi* (*David*) (+ OE *stów*), '*holy place*'

Daw's House, (E, C17), Dawe's House, '*Dawe family's house*'

Degembris (*Tykambret* n.d.), Tycambres, '*Cambret's manor*'

Degibna (*S. Degamannus* 1427), Degaman, '*St Decuman('s chapel)*'

Delabole (*Delyou Bol* 1284), Delyow Bol, '*pit at Delyow ('place of leaves')*'

Delamere (*Delyoumur* 1284), Delyow Muer, '*great Delyow*'

De Lank (*Dynlonk* C16), Dinlonk, '*ravine fort*'

Delinuth (*Delyownewyth* 1296), Delyow Nowyth, '*new Delyow*'

Demelza (*Dynmaelda* 1309), Dinmalsa, '*Maelda's fort*'

Denzell (*Dynesel* C12), Dinasel, '*little fort*'

Derval (*Deverell* 1323), Devrel, '*watery place*'

Deveral, Devrel, '*watery place*'

Devichoys (*Kilcoys* 1652; *Deviscoys* 1652), Kilcoos, Tevyscoos, '*ridge wood; plantation wood*'

Deviock (*Deviek* 1311), ?an Devyek, ?'*the cultivated place/stream*'

Devoran (*Devrian* 1522), Devrion, '*waters*'

Dimson (OE, *Dynysham* 1327), Dynisham, '*Dynni's river meadow*'

Dinas, Dinas, '*fort*'

Dizzard (*Dysert* 1238), Disert (OC), '*very steep*'

Dobwalls (E, *Dobbewalles* 1619), Dobb's Walls, '*Dobbe family's walls*'

Doddycross (E, *Doddacrosse* 1516), Dodda's Cross, '*Dodda family's cross*'

Dolcoath, ?Dorcoth, ?'*old ground*'

Dolphin Town (Scilly), Godholcan, (*after Godolphin family*)

Domellick (*Dynmyliek* 1284), Din Mylyek, '*Milioc's fort*'

Dorminack, Dormeynek, '*stony ground*'

Doublebois (F, *Dobelboys* 1293), Doublebois, '*two-part wood*'

Dowha (*Dyuuer* 1317), Dowr, '*stream*'

Downderry (E, C17), ?Downdairy, ?'*hill dairy*'

Downgate (Linkinh.) (*Caradon Yet* 1428), Yet Carn, '*gate to Caradon*'

Downgate (Stoke Climsl.) (E, C18), Down Gate, '*gate to a hill*'

Downhill (St Eval) (E, C18), Down Hill, '*downland hill*'

Downinney (OE, *Downeny* 1356), Downeny, (?*meaning*)

Dowran, Dowran, '*watering place*'

Drakewalls (E, C19), Drake's Walls, '*Drake family's walls*'

Drannack (*Dreynek* 1284), Dreynek, '*thorny*'

Drawbridge (*Drafurde* 1492; OE, *dræg ford*), Dragford, '*drag-slope ford*'

Draynes (*Draynez* C13), Dreynys, '*thorn-brake*'

Drewollas (*Trewollas* 1655), Trewoles, '*lower farm*'

Drift, Higher (*Drefmur* 1327), an Drev Veur, '*great Drift*'

Drift, Lower (*Drefbyghan* 1262), an Drev Vian, '*little Drift ('farm')*'

Drinnick (S. Petherwin) (*Dreynek* 1582), Dreynek, '*thorny*'

Drinnick (St Stephen) (*Dreynek* 1370), Dreynek, '*thorny*'

Drym (*Drym* c. 1180), Drumm, '*ridge*'

Duloe (*Dewlo* 1504), Dewlogh, '*two Looe rivers*'; (*Lankyp* 1286), Lan Gyby, '*St Kybi's church site*'

Dunheved (OE, *Dunhevet* 1086–1584, *Dounhed* C11), Donheved, '*head of a hill*'

Dunmere (*Dynmur* 1220), Dinmeur, '*large fort*'

Dupath (*Thieuespath* 1195; OE, *péofa pæð*), Thievespath, '*thieves' path*'

Duporth (*Deuborth* 1338), Dewborth, '*two coves*'

Durfold (*Dyrfold* c. 1580; OE, *déor fold*, Deerfold, '*deer fold*'

Durgan (*Dourgen* 1813), Dowrgeun, '*place of otters*'

Dutson (*Dodeston* 1281; OE, *Doddes tún*), Dodston, '*Dodda's farm*'

Eastcott (OE, *be éastan cote*), Eastcot, '*east of the cottage*'

Eathorne (*Eytron* 1392, *Ethron* 1417), Eytron, Ethron, (*?meaning*)

Edgcumbe (E), Edgcome, '*Edgcome family*'

Edmonton (E, C19), Edmundston, '*Edmund Hambley's settlement*'

Eggbear (OE, *ecg bearu*), Egbear, '*hillside grove*'

Eglarooze (*Eglosros* 1360), Eglos Ros, '*church of the Rame peninsula*'

Egloshayle (*Eglosheyl* 1197), Eglos Heyl, '*church on the Hayle river*'

Egloskerry (*Egloskery* c. 1145), Eglos Kery, '*St Keri's church*'

Elerkey (*Elerghy* 1349), Elerhy, '*place of swans*'

Ellbridge (OE, *Thelebrigge* 1324), Thelbridge, '*plank bridge*'

Ellenglaze (*Elynglas* 1302), Elyn Glas, '*green Elyn (stream name, 'bend')*'

Embla (*Emle* 1301), Amal, '*slope, boundary (stream name)*'

Engelley (*Gilly* 1404), an Gelly, '*the grove*'

Engollan (*Hengollen* 1418), Hengollen, '*old hazel tree*'

Ennestreven (*Enestreven* 1683), Enystreven, '*isolated place with houses*'

Ennis, Enys, '*isolated/remote place*'

Enniscaven (*Enyscawen* 1472), Enysscawen, '*isolated area with an elder tree*'

Ennisworgey (*Enisworgy* 1332), Enysworgy, '*Wurci's isolated land*'

Ennys (*Enys* 1438), Enys, '*isolated, remote*'

Enys, Enys, '*isolated, remote*'

Erisey (*Erysy* 1284), Erysy, '*ploughland place*'

Erth (OE, *ierð*), Yerth, '*ploughland*'

Escalls (*Eskeles* 1281), Ascalys, '*place of thistles*'

Fairy Cross (E, *Faircros* 1359), Fair Cross, '*fair cross*'

Falmouth (E, C13), Arwennek, '*facing the white one (stream)*'; Loghfala, Aberfala, Falmeth, '*estuary of the Fal*'

Farms Common (E), Farms Common, '*common grazing between farms*'

Faugan (*Fawgan* 1689), Fowgan, '*white/fair beeches*'

Fawton (*Fawiton* 1205), Fowy, '*beech-trees river*' (+ OE *tún*, '*farm*')

Fentonadle (*Fentonadwen* C13), Fenten Adwyn, '*St Adwyn's well*'

Fentongollan (*Fentengollen* 1201), Fenten Gollen, '*hazel-tree spring*'

Fentonluna (*Fenton-leno* 1552), Fenten Lenow, '*spring by strip-fields*'

Fenton Pitts (*Fenton* 1340), Fenten, '*spring, well*'

Feock (*Lanfioc c.* 1165; *La Vague*, mod.), Lanviok, '*St Feoc's church site*'

Fernsplatt (E), Fernsplot, '*plot of land with ferns*'

Fiddler's Green (E), Fiddler's Green, '*fiddler's green*'

Five Lanes (E), Five Lanes, '*where five lanes meet*'

Fletchersbridge (E, C18), Flegard's Bridge, '*Flegard family's bridge*'

Flexbury (OE, *fleax byrig*), Flaxbyry, '*fort where flax grows*'

Flushing (Mylor) (*Nankersis* 1590), Nanskersys, '*reed-grown valley*'

Flushing (St Anthony in Meneage) (D), Vlissingen, (*after Vlissingen, SW Netherlands*)

Foage (*Bos* 1315), Bos, '*dwelling*'

Fonston (E, *Faunteston* 1284), Fauntston, '*Faunte family's farm*'

Forda (*Forde* 1442; ME) *atte forde*), Atford, '*at the ford*'

Forder (OE, *æt þæm forde*), Atford, '*at the ford*'

Forge (E), Forge, '*forge*'

Forrabury (OE, *Forbyri* 1291), Forebyry, '*in front of a fort*'

Four Lanes (E, C18), Four Lanes, '*where four lanes meet*'

Fowey (*Fawi c.* 1200), Fowy, '*beech-trees river*'; (*Langorthou* 1310), Langordhow, '*clans' church site*'

Foxhole (E, C17), Foxhole, '*fox's hollow*'

Fraddam, For' Adam, '*Adam's road*'

Fraddon (*Frodan* 1321), Frodan (OC), '*stream place*'

Freathy (E, *Vridie* 1286)), Fridia, '*Fridia family*'

Frogpool (E, C19), Frogpool, '*frogs' pool*'

Frogwell (OE, *froggana wielle*), Frogwell, '*frogs' stream/spring*'

Frythens (*Breghtyn* 1306), Breghtyn, '*dappled rounded hill*'

Fursdon (OE, *fyrs dún*), Furzedon, '*furze hill*'

Fursnewth (*Fosneweth* 1196), Fosnowyth, '*new wall/bank*'

Furzenapp (*Vorsknapp* 1365; OE, *fyrs cnæpp*), Furzeknapp, '*furze hill*'

Gadles, an Gadlys (OC), '*the bailey/military HQ*'

Galowras (*Golowres* 1428), Golowres, '*sunlight watercourse*'

Gam (*Caam* 1351), Camm, '*bend*'

Gang (E C19, mining dialect), Gang, '*gang*'

Gargus (*Cargus* 1334), Cargos, Kergos, '*fort at a wood*'

Garker (*Karker* 1354), Carhar, '*shackle, lock-up, stocks*'

Garlenick (*Corlennek* 1334), Corlenek, '*hedge by a strip-field system*'

Garlidna (*Gerlynnow* 1461), Grelydnow, '*stock ponds*'

Garras (*Garros c.* 1320), Gar'ros, '*rugged roughland*'

Gaverigan (*Govergwyn* 1302), Govergwynn, '*white stream*'

Gear (Camborne) (*Kaervran* 1283), Ker Vran, '*crow's/Bran's fort*'

Gear (Madron) (*Caer* 1323), Ker, '*fort*'

Gear (Mawgan) (*Caer* 1086), Ker, '*fort*'

Gear (St Erth) (*Kaer* 1386), Ker, '*fort*'

Gear (Zennor) (*Kaer* 1327), Ker, '*fort*'

Georgia (*The Gorga Croft c.* 1696), Croft an Gor Ge, '*rough grazing of the low/broken-down hedge*'

Germoe (*Germogh* 1289), Germogh, '*St Germoch*'

Gernick (*Kernic* 1229), Kernyk, '*little corner*'

Gerrans (*Gerens* 1584), Gerens, '*St Gerent*'

Gew (*Kew* 1456), Kew, '*paddock, enclosure, hollow*'

Gilbert's Coombe (E), Gilbert's Cumb, '*Gilbert family's valley*'

Gillan (*Gillyn* 1327, *Killian* 1507), Kilen, '*creek, inlet*'

Gilly Gabben (*Kyllygam* 1506), Kellygabm, '*crooked grove*'

Gillywartha, Kelly Wartha, '*higher grove*'

Glasdon (*Glazon* 1748), Glasen, '*greensward*'

Glasney (*Glasneyth* 1291), Glasneth, '*verdure*'

Glendurgan (mod.), Glynn Dowrgeun, '*deep valley at Durgan*'

Gloweth (*Glowyth* 1485), Glowwedh, '*trees that supply charcoal*'

Gluvian (*Glyvion* 1293), Glyvyan, (?*meaning*)

Glynn (*Glyn* 1351), Glynn, '*deep valley*'

Godolphin (*Godholkan c.* 1210), Godholcan, '*tin-stream*'

Godrevy, Godrevy, '*homesteads*'

Goenrounsan, Goon Ronsyn, '*ass's downs*'

Golant (*Golenance* 1454), Golnans, '*festival valley*'

Golberdon (OE, *golde burna dún*), Goldburndon, '*hill by a marigold stream*'

Golden (*Wolvadon* 1327; OE, *wulfa dún*), Wolfdon, '*wolf hill*'; (*Trewygran* C12), Trewygran, (?*meaning*)

Goldsithney (*Golsythny* 1410), Golsydhny, '(*place of*) St Sithni's feast*'

Gollawater (*Golleyth* 1329, *Angolleth* 1720), an Gollwedh, '*the hazel trees*'

Gonamena (*Gunnemaine* 1473), Gonyow Meyn, '*downs of stones*'

Gonvena (*Gwynveneth* 1286), Gwynveneth, '*white/fair-hillside*'

Goodagrane (*Gothowgran* 1451), Godhowgran, '*bracken/scrub streams*'

Goonabarn (*Goenbaren* 1564), Goon Baren, (?*meaning*)

Goonamarris (*Guenenmarges* 1290), Goon an Marghes, '*the horses' downs*'

Goonamarth (*Goenenmargh* 1345), Goon an Margh, '*the horse's downs*'

Goonbell, Goon Bell, '*far downs*'

Goongillings (*Goon Gillin* 1649), Goon Gilen, '*creek downs*'

Goonhavern (*Goenhavar* 1290), Goon Havar, '*downs of summer fallow*'

Goonhingey (*Goynhensy* 1342), Goon Henjy, '*downs with an old/ruined house*'

Goonhoskyn, Goon Heskyn, '*sedge downs*'

Goonhusband, Goon Hosebond, '*downs of the Hosebond family*'

Gooninis (*Goenenys* 1404), Goon Enys, '*isolated downs*'

Goonlaze (St Agnes) (*Goonlas c.* 1720), Goon Las, '*green downs*'

Goonlaze (Stithians), Goon Las, *'green downs'*

Goonown (*Gooneowne* 1612), Goon Own, ?*'downs of fear'*

Goon Piper, Goon Pyper, Goon Piber, *'Piper family's downs'*

Goonreeve (*Gonruth* 1613), Goon Rudh, *'red downs'*

Goonvares, Goon Weras, *'slope downs'*

Goonvean (Kenwyn), Goon Vian, *'little downs'*

Goonvean (Stithians), Goon Vian, *'little downs'*

Goonvrea, Goon Vre, *'hill downs'*

Goonwin, Goon Wynn, *'white downs'*

Goonzion, Goon Sehen, *'waterless downs'*

Gooseford (OE, *gós ford*), Gooseford, *'goose ford'*

Gooseham (OE, *gós hamm*), Gooseham, *'river-meadow of geese'*

Gormellick (*Gonmaylek* 1327), Goon Mailek, *'Maeloc's downs'*

Gorran (*Langoron* 1373, *Laworran* 1717), Lanworon, *'St Goron's church site'*

Gorrangorras (*Goneangoras* C16), Goon an Gores, *'downs at the weir/dam'*

Gorran Haven (*Porteuste* 1576), Porth Ust, *'St Just's cove'*

Goscott (OE, *Godescot* 1238), Godascot, *'Goda's cottage'*

Gothers (*Gothfos* 1334), Goothfos, *'stream-wall'*

Goverseth, Goversegh, *'stream that dries in summer'*

Grade, Grad, *'St Grada'*

Grambla (Wendron) (*Cromlegh* 1327), Cromlegh, *'dolmen'*

Grambler (Gwennap) (*Gromleth* c. 1610), an Gromlegh, *'the dolmen'*

Grampound (F, *Graundpont* 1401), Grandpont, *'large bridge'*; (*Ponsmur* 1296), Pons Muer, *'large bridge'*

Grampound Road (E, C19), Grandpont Road, *'road to Grampound'*

Gready (*Gredyou* 1400), Grediow, *'stock sheds'*

Greenbottom (E, C19), Green Bottom, *'green valley bottom'*

Greensplat (E, *The Green Plot* 1754), Greensplat, *'green plot'*

Greenwith Common (*Grenwyth* 1480), an Grenwydh, *'the aspen trees'*

Gregwartha, Crug Wartha, *'higher barrow'*

Greystone Bridge (OE, *grég stán*), Greystone Bridge, *'bridge at Greystone'*

Griglands, Gruglon, *'clump of heather'*

Grillis (*Grelles* 1302), an Grellas, *'the ruined huts'*

Grimsby, New (Scilly) (O.Sc., *Grimrs ey*), New Grimsey, *'new Grim's island'*

Grimsby, Old (Scilly) (O.Sc.), Old Grimsey, *'old Grim's island'*

Grimscott (OE), Grimscot, *'Grim's cottage'*

Grogarth or **Grogoth** (*Crugoyt* 1278), Crug Cuit (OC), *'barrow in a wood'*

Grugwith or **Grugith** (*Crukwaeth* 967), Crug Wedh, *'trees barrow'*

Grumbla (*Gromlogh* 1498), an Gromlegh, *'the dolmen'*

Gulval (*Lanystly* 1328), Lanystly, *'Ystli's church site'* (Gulval < St Gwolvela)

Gummow's Shop (E, C17), Gummow's Shop, *'Gummow family's workshop'*

Gunheath (*Goenheth* 1310), Goon Hedh, *'red deer's downs'*

Gunnislake (*Gunnalake* 1608; OE, *Gunna lacu*), Gunnalake, *'Gunna's stream'*

Gunvenna (*Goenfynou* 1275), Goon Finow, '*boundaries downs*'

Gunwalloe (*Wynwola* 1499), Wynwalo, '*St Winwalo*'; (*Gwynyon* 1439), Gwynen, '*white place*'

Gunwalloe Fishing Cove, Porth Wynwalo, '*St Wynwalo's cove*'

Gunwen (*Goynwen* 1483), Goon Wenn, '*white downs (fem. of* gwynn)'

Gurland (*Gorlyn* 1284), an Gorlyn, '*the sheepfold*'

Gwallon (*Wallen* 1338, *Gwallan* 1415), Gwallyn, '*little wall*'

Gwarder (*Gwerthour* 1312), Gwer'-dhowr, '*green water/stream*'

Gwarnick (*Gwernek c.* 1400), Gwernek, '*alder-grove*'

Gwarth-an-drea, Gwarth an Dre, '*high part of the settlement*'

Gwavas (Grade), Gwavos, '*winter farm*'

Gwavas (Paul), Gwavos, '*winter farm*'

Gwavas (Sithney), Gwavos, '*winter farm*'

Gwealavellan (*Gweal-la-vellan* 1736), ?Gwel an Velyn, '*the mill field*'

Gwealdues (*Gweale due* 1691), Gwel Du, '*dark/black field*'

Gwealeath (*Guaenelegh* 1288), Goon Legh, '*slab downs*'

Gwealmellin, Gwel Melyn, '*mill field*'

Gwedna (*Gwenna* 1409), Gwedna, '*white/fair one (stream name)*'

Gweek (*Gwyk* 1358, *Gweege c.*1700), Gwig, '*forest settlement*'

Gwendra (*Gwyndreth* 1343), Gwyndreth, '*white-beach*'

Gwendreath (*Gwyndraeth* 1346), Gwyndreth, '*white-beach*'

Gwennap (*Lanwenap* 1328), Lanwenap, '*St Wenap's church site*'

Gwennymoor (E), Gwynnow Moor, '*Gwynnow family's marsh*'

Gwenter (*Gwynter* 1519), Gwyntir, '*white/fair-land*'

Gwills (*Gwyllis* 1335), Gwyles, '(*place of*) *lovage*'

Gwinear (*Gwynier* 1584), Gwynyer, '*St Gwinier*'

Gwithian (*Gothyan* 1535, *Gwythyen* 1567), Gwydhyan, '*St Guedian*'

Hailglower or **Halgolluir**, Helyglowarth, Helyglowar', '*willow garden*'

Halabezack (*Halwebesek* 1338), Halwebesek, '*gnat-infested marsh*'

Halamanning (*Halemanyn* 1651), Halamanen, '*marsh by lush pasture*'

Halangy (Scilly) (*Hallingey* 1910), Hallynjy, '*pool-house marsh*'

Halbullock (*Halbohek* 1338), Halbothek, '*humped marsh*'

Hale Mills, Melynhal, '*marsh mill*'

Halgabron (*Halgybran* 1303), Halgigbran, '*carrion-crow's marsh*'

Hall (*Halle* 1401; OE, *æt þæm hale*), Hale, '*at the nook*'

Hallaze (*Halelase* 1503), Hallas, '*green marsh*'

Hallew, Hallow, '*marshes*'

Halligye (*Heligy* 1284), Helygy, '*place/stream of willows*'

Hallworthy (*Halworgy* 1415), Halworgy, '*Wurci's marsh*'; (*Haldronket* 1415), Haldroncuit (OC), '*hillspur-wood marsh*'

Halsetown (E, C19), Halse Town, '*settlement built by James Halse*'

Halton Barton (*Healton* 1214; OE, *healh tún*), Halton, '*farm on a river bend*'

Halvana (*Hyrmene* 1194), Hirmene', '*long-hillside*'

Halvosso (*Hafossowe* 1532), Havosow, *'summer farms, shielings'*

Halwin, Halwynn, *'white/fair marsh'*

Halwinnick, Halwynnek, *'marsh by the stream called Gwynnek'*

Halwyn (St Issey) (*Helwyn* 1259), Helwynn, *'white/fair hall'*

Halzephron (*Alseyeffarn* 1488), Als Yfarn, *'hell cliff'*

Hammett (*Hamet* 1086), Havod (OC), *'shieling, summer grazing'*

Hampt (*Havet* 1338), Havod (OC), *'shieling, summer grazing'*

Hannafore (OE, *Henofer* 1642, *Hanaver* 1654), Hanafair, *'cock fair/market'*

Hantergantick (*Handregantek* 1296), Hendre Gantek, *'home farm on border-land'*

Hantertavis (*Hantertavas* 1522), Hantertavas, *'(rock shaped like) half a tongue'*

Harcourt (*Harcrack* C13), Arcrak, *'facing a crag'*

Harewood (*Hergarth* 1351), Hiryarth, *'long ridge'*

Harlyn (*Arlyn* 1334), Arlyn, *'facing a pool'*

Harrowbarrow (OE, *Harebeare* 1313), Harebear, *'hare's grove'*

Harrowbridge (ME, *Horebregge* 1220), Horbridge, *'grey bridge'*

Hatt (OE, *hæt*), Hat, *'hat-shaped hill'*

Hay (St Breock), (OE, *gehæg*), Hay, *'enclosure, holding'*

Haye (Callington) (OE, *gehæg*), Hay, *'enclosure/holding'*

Hayle (*Heyl* 1265), Heyl, *'estuary with tidal flats'*

Heamoor (*Anhaye* 1619), an Hay, *'the enclosure'*

Hele (Bude) (*La Hayle* 1250), Heyl, *'estuary with tidal flats'*

Hele (Jacobstow) (*Hele* 1196; OE, *healh*), Heal, *'nook, corner of land'*

Helebridge (*Ponteheale* 1662), Pontheyl, (OC), *'bridge at Hele'*

Helford (*Hayleford* 1318), Heyl, *'inlet with tidal flats'*

Helford Passage (*Haylford Treath* n.d.), Treth Heyl, *'ferry to Helford'*

Heligan, Helygen, *'willow tree'*

Helland (Bodmin), Henlan, *'disused church site'*

Helland (Mabe), Henlan, *'disused church site'*

Helland (Probus), Henlan, *'disused church site'*

Helland (St Teath) (OE, *Haylond* 1345), Hayland, Highland, *'land used for growing hay', 'high land'*

Hellandbridge, Pons Henlan, *'bridge at Helland'*

Hellangove, Hel an Gov, *'Angove's (the smith's) hall'*

Hellescott (*Hilscote* 1330; OE), Hilscot, ?**Hielle's cottage'*

Hellesvean, Henlys Vian, *'little Henlys ('old ruin')'*

Hellesveor, Henlys Veur, *'great Henlys ('old ruin')'*

Helscott (*Hillevescot* 1253; OE, *hyll efes cot*), Hillevescot, *'cottage on a hill-brow'*

Helston (*Henlistone* 1086, *Hellys* 1396), Henlys, *'old court/ruin'*

Helston Water, Dowr Henlys, *'stream at Helston'*

Helstone (*Henliston* 1086), Henlys, *'old court/ruin'*

Helvear (Scilly) (*Hayle Veor* C16), Heyl Veur, *'large inlet with tidal flats'*

Hendersick (*Hendresuk* 1314), Hendresegh, Hendresygh, '*waterless home farm*'

Hendra (Breage), Hendre, '*home farm*'

Hendra (Camelford), Hendre, '*home farm*'

Hendra (Ladock), Hendre, '*home farm*'

Hendra (Ruan Major), Hendre, '*home farm*'

Hendra (St Dennis), Hendre, '*home farm*'

Hendra (St Ives), Hendre, '*home farm*'

Hendra (St Just), Hendre, '*home farm*'

Hendra (St Teath), Hendre, '*home farm*'

Hendra (Sancreed), Hendre, '*home farm*'

Hendra (Stithians), Hendre, '*home farm*'

Hendra (Wendron), Hendre, '*home farm*'

Hendra (Withiel), Hendre, '*home farm*'

Hendrabridge (*Hendrabrigge* 1418), Hendre, '*home farm*' (*with addition of* ME *brigge*)

Hendraburnick (*Hendrebrunnek* 1296), Hendrebronnck, '*home farm by a rush-bed*'

Hendra Croft (Perranzabuloe) (*Hendre* 1327), Hendra, '*home farm*'

Hendravossan (*Hendrefosen* 1479), Hendrefosyn, '*home farm at a little wall/ bank*'

Hendrifton (*Hendreneythyn* 1362), Hendre'n Eythyn, '*home farm at the furze*'

Henmoor (*Hyndemor* 1261; OE, *hinde mór*), Hindmoor, '*hind's marsh*'

Henwood (OE, *henn wudu*), Henwood, '*hens' wood*'

Herland (*Hyrleyn* 1283), Hirlen, '*long strip-field*'

Herniss (*Hyrnans* 1290), Hirnans, '*long-vale*'

Herodsfoot, Benhiryard (OC), '*foot of a long ridge*'

Herodshead (*Bronhiriard* 1284), Bronhiryard (OC), '*long-ridge hill*'

Hersham (*Hesham* 1355; OE, *hæs hamm*), Hesham, '*brushwood enclosure*'

Heskyn, Heskyn, '*sedge*'

Hessenford (OE, *hægtsena ford*), Hagsenford, '*hags' ford*'

Hewas Water, Dowr Havos, '*shieling/ summer farm stream*'

Hick's Mill (E), Hick's Mill, '*Hick family's mill*'

High Cross (Constantine) (E), High Cross, '*high cross*'

High Lanes (Hayle) (E), High Lanes, '*high lanes*'

High Lanes (Gorran) (E), High Lanes, '*high lanes*'

High Street (E, C18), High Street, '*principal street*'

Higher Bal, Bal Wartha, '*higher mine working*'

Higher Condurrow (*Kendorou* 1327), Kendowrow Wartha, '*upper junction of streams*'

Higher Downs (*Goon Sent Eler c.* 1680), Goon Sent Eler, '*St Hilary Downs*'

Higher Tolcarne, Talcarn Wartha, '*higher Talcarn ('brow-tor')*'

Higher Town (Roche) (E), Higher Town, '*higher farm*'

Higher Tremarcoombe, Comtrevargh Wartha, '*higher Tremar valley*'

Highertown (Truro) (E), Higher Town, '*higher settlement*'

Highertown (Advent) (E), Higher Town, '*higher farm*'

Highway (Redruth) (E), Highway, '*highway*'

Holmbush (E, C18 from OE, *holegn bysca*), Holnbush, '*holly bush*'

Holwood (ME, *Holewode* 1263) Holewood, *'hollow wood'*

Holy Vale (Scilly) (OF, *La Val* 1301) La Val, *'low-lying'*

Holywell (E), Holy Well, *'holy well'*

Honicombe (OE, *hunig cumb*), Honeycombe, *'honey valley'*

Hornick, Hornek, *'iron-like (soil?)'*

Hornifast (OE, *Herdenefast* 1200), Herdenfast, *'herdsmen's stronghold'*

Horningtops (OE, *horning top*), Horningtop, *'top of a horn-shaped hill'*

Horsebridge (ME or MF, *Hautes Brygge* 1437), Hautes Bridge, *?'Haute's bridge'*

Horsedowns (E, C18 *Horse Down*), Horse Down, *'horse down'*

Hugh Town (Scilly) (*Hue* 1708; OE, *hóh*), Hoe, *'heel of land'*

Hugus, Ughgos, *'high-wood'*

Hustyn (ME, *Husting* 1243), Husting, *'assembly house'*

Huthnance, Heuthnans, *'pleasant valley'*

Idless (*Ethelys* 1504), Edhelys, *'place of aspens'*

Illand (OE, *Eyllalande* 1284), Eyllaland, *'Aella's land'*

Illogan (*Egloshallow* 1700), Eglos Hallow, *'marshes church'*

Illogan Highway, Fordh Yllogan, *'road to Illogan'*

Inchs (E, *Inch's Spring* 1948), Inch's Spring, *'Inch family's spring'*

Indian Queens (E, *Indian Queen c.* 1870), Indian Queen, (*C19 inn name*)

Innis (*Enys* 1554), Enys, *'isolated land'*

Innisvath, Enysvargh, *'horse's/Meirch's isolated land'*

Inow (*Iwenau* 1269), Ewenow, *'yew trees'*

Insworke (*Eniswork* 1361), Enys, *'island'* (+ OE *geweorc*, *'earthworks'*)

Jacobstow (OE, *Jacobes stów*), Jacobstow, *'St Jacob's (James's) holy place'*

Jolly's Bottom (E), Jolly's Bottom, *'Jolly family's valley bottom'*

Joppa (Hayle), Shoppa, *'workshop'*

Joppa (St Just), Shoppa, *'workshop'*

Kaledna (*Kelennou* 1315), Kelydnow, *'holly trees'*

Karslake (OE, *cærse lacu*), Cresslake, *'cress stream'*

Kea, Ke, *'St Kei'*

Kea, old (*Landegei* 1184), Landege, *'thy St Kei's church site'*

Keason (OE, *Kestyngton* 1175), Kestington, *'farm of Cæst's people'*

Kehelland (*Kellyhellan* 1284), Kellyhenlan, *'grove at Henlan ('disused churchsite')'*

Keigwin (*Keguyn* 1302–1539, *Kiguidden* 1676), Kegwydn, *'white hedge'*

Kellow (*Kelyou* 1302), Kelliow, *'groves'*

Kelly, Kelly, *'grove'*

Kelly Bray (*Kellibregh c.* 1286), Kellybregh, *'dappled grove'*

Kellygreen (*Keligren* 1258), Kellygren, *'aspen grove'*

Kelynack, Kelynek, *'holly grove'*

Kemyel (*Kemyel* 1283–1427), Kemyel, (*?meaning*)

Kenegie (*Kenegy* 1259), Keunegy, *'reedbeds'*

Kenidjack (*Kenygiek* 1326), Keunyjek, *'land used for fuel-gathering'*

Kennacott (E, *Hennacote c.* 1840), Hennacot, *'Henna's cottage'*

Kennard's House (E), Kennard's House, *'Kennard family's house'*

Kenneggy, Keunegy, *'reed-beds'*

Kenneggy Downs, Goon Geunegy, *'downs at Kenneggy'*

Kents (E, *Kents Hill c.* 1840), Kente's Hill, *'Kente family's hill'*

Kenwyn (*Keynwyn* 1316), Keynwynn, *'white/fair ridge'*

Kergilliack (*Kegulyek* 1327), Kegulyek, *'cockerel's hedge'*

Kerley (*Crugbleth* 1306), Crug Bleydh, *'wolf's barrow'*

Kernewas (*Kynyavos* 1513), Kynyavos, *'autumn dwelling'*

Kernick (St Stephen) (*Kernek* 1327), Kernyk, *'little corner'*

Kernock (*Kernek* 1302), Kernyk, *'little corner'*

Kerris (*Kerrys* 1440), Kerys, *'fort-place'*

Kerrow (Blisland) (*Cayrou* 1356, *Kerow c.* 1580), Kerrow, *'forts'*

Kerrow (Morvah) (*Cayrou* 1327), Kerrow, *'forts'*

Kerrow (St Austell) (*Cayrou* 1327), Kerrow, *'forts'*

Kerrow (St Erth) (*Cayrou* 1329), Kerrow, *'forts'*

Kerrow (St Just) (Kerowe 1589), Kerrow, *'forts'*

Kerrowe (Zennor) (Nancarrow 1738), Nanscarow, *'stag's valley'*

Kersbrook Cross (OE, *cærse bróc*), Kersbrook, *'cress stream'*

Kerslake (OE, *cærse lacu*), Cresslake, *'cress stream'*

Kerthen (Kerthyn 1284), Kerdhyn, *'rowan tree'*

Kestle (St Columb Major) (*Castel* 1194), Castel, *'castle, fort'*

Kestle (St Ewe), Castel, *'castle, fort'*

Kestle Mill (*Castel* 1194), Melyn Gastel, *'mill at Kestle ('castle, fort')'*

Keveral (*Keverel* 1299), Kevarel, *'place of joint-tillage'*

Keybridge (OE, *cý brycg*), Cybridge; Cowbridge, *'cow's bridge'*

Keyrse (*Keuros c.* 1150), Kewros, *'hollow-roughland'*

Kilgogue (*Kelligog* 1235), Kellygog, *'cuckoo grove'*

Kilhallon (*Kellyhon c.* 1180), Kellyon, *'ash grove'*

Kilkhampton (*Kelk c.* 839), Kelgh, Kylgh, *'circle, ring'*

Killaganogue (*Killignowek* 1388), Kellygnowek, *'nut-producing grove'*

Killaworgey (*Kylworge c.* 1320), Kilworgy, *'Wurci's ridge'*

Killifreth (*Kellyvregh* 1345), Kellyvregh, *'dappled grove'*

Killiganoon (*Kellygnohan* 1291), Kellygnowen, *'nut grove'*

Killigarth (*Kylgath* 1214), Kilgath, *'cat's ridge'*

Killigrew (*Kelligreu* 1175–1378), Kellygrew, *'grove at a weir'*

Killiow, Kellyow, *'groves'*

Killiserth, Kellyserth, *'steep grove'*

Killivose (St Allen) (*Kylvos* 1314), Kilvos, *'ridge with a wall/bank'*

Killivose (Camborne) (*Kyllyvos* 1480), Kellyvos, *'wall grove'*

Kilmarth (*Kylmergh* 1329), Kilmergh, *'horses' ridge'*

Kilminant (*Kylmenaunt* 1476), Kilmenawed (OC), *'awl-shaped ridge'*

Kilquite (*Kylguit* 1327), Kilcuit (OC), *'wood ridge'*

Kingbath (*Kynburgh* 1427), Kingburgh, *'king's barrow'*

Kingbeare (OE, *cyne bearu*), Kingbear, *'royal grove'*

Kingsand (E, C17), King's Sand, *'King family's beach'*

Kingston (OE, *Kyenestone* 1317), Cyneston, *'Cyne's farm'*

Kirland (*Crellen* 1302), Crenlyn, *'aspens pool'*

Knatterbury (E, *Nattle bury c.* 1840), Nettlebyry, *'nettles fort'*

Knightsmill (E, *Kenystesmylle* 1306), Knight's Mill, *'knight's mill'*

Kuggar (*Coger* 1324), Coger, *'winding (stream name)'*

Kynance (*Keynance* 1620), Keynans, *'ravine'*

Laddenvean (*Lanvyghan* 1369), Ladn Vian, *'little church site'*

Ladock (*Egloslagek* 1354), Eglos Lajek, *'St Ladoca's church'*

Laity, Lety, *'dairy'*

Laity Moor, Goon Lety, *'dairy downs'*

Lamanva (*Lamanva* 1390), Lamanva, (*?meaning*)

Lambessow (*Lanbedou* 1308), Lanbesow, *'birch-trees enclosure'*

Lambourne (*Lanbron* 1231), Lanbronn, *'hill enclosure'*

Lamellion (*Nansmelin* 1298), Nans Melyn, *'mill valley'*

Lamellyn (*Nansmelyn* 1296), Nans Melyn, *'mill valley'*

Lamellyon, Nans Melyn, *'mill valley'*

Lammana (*Lamana* 1300), Lanmanagh, *'monk's church enclosure'*

Lamorick (*Lamorek* 1406), Nans Morek, *'Moroc's valley'*

Lamorna (*Nansmorno* 1302), Nans Mornow, *'valley of the Morno (stream name)'*

Lamorran (*Lanmoren* 1187), Lanmoren, *'Moren's church site'*

Lampen (*Lanpen* 1250), ?Nans Penn, *?'end valley'*

Lanarth (St Keverne) (*Lannergh* 1357), Lannergh, *'clearing'*

Lancarrow (*Nanscarou* 1338), Nans Carow, *'stag's valley'*

Landlooe, Nant Logh (OC), *'valley of the Looe river'*

Land's End (*Pen an ulays* 1504; pre-occlusion from *c.* 1680), Pedn an Wlas, *'end of the land'*

Landewednack (*Landewynnec* 1290), Landewydnek, *'thy St Winnoc's church site'*

Landrake (*Lanrach* 1291), Lannergh, *'clearing'*

Landrivick (*Hendrevyk* 1324), Hendrevyk, *'little home farm'*

Landue (*Landu c.* 1210), ?Nantdu (OC), *'dark valley'*

Landulph (*Landelech* 1086; *Landhylp* 1311), Landhelek, *'St Deloc's church site'*

Lane (E), Lane, *'lane'*

Laneast (*Lanayst c.* 1226), Lanayst, (*?meaning*)

Lane-end (E), Lane End, *'end of a lane'*

Lanescot (*Lisnestec c.* 1180), Lysnestek, *'Nestoc's court'*

Langarth (*Lenengath* 1365), Lenangath, *'the cat's strip-field'*

Langdon (OE, *Langedon* 1201), Langdon, *'long hill'*

Langford (OE, *Langeford* 1321), Langford, *'long ford'*

Langore (*Langover* 1431), Nans Gover, *'stream valley'*

Langunnett (*Langenewit* 1086), Langenewyt (OC), *'Cyneuit's church enclosure'*

Lanhydrock (*Lanhidrok* 1299), Lanhydrek, *'Hidroc's church site'*

44

Lanivet (*Lanneves* 1301), Lanneves, '*church site by a sacred grove*'

Lanjeth (*Nansyrgh* 1356), Nans Yergh, '*roebucks' valley*'

Lanjew (Kea) (*Nansciu c.* 1260), Nans Kiogh, '*snipe valley*'

Lanjew (Withiel) (*Lendu* 1356), Lendu, '*dark strip-field*'

Lank (*Lonc* 1303), Lonk, '*ravine*'

Lanlawren (*Nanslowarn* 1356), Nans Lowarn, '*fox valley*'

Lanlivery (*Lanlyvri c.* 1170), Lanlyvry, '*Lyfri's church site*'

Lannarth (*Lannargh* 1413), Lannergh, '*clearing*'

Lanner (*Lanergh* 1302), Lannergh, '*clearing*'

Lanreath (*Lanredoch* 1086, *Lanreythou* 1266), Lanreydhek, '*Reidoc's church site*'

Lansallos (*Lansalwys* 1326), Lansalwys, '*Salwed's church site*'

Lanseague (*Nansceueguy* 1321), Nans Ewigy, '*hinds' valley*'

Lantallack (*Lantollek* 1329), Nant Tollek (OC), '*hollowed valley*'

Lanteague (*Lanleke* 1452), ?Nans Legh, ?'*slab valley*'

Lanteglos (*Nanteglos* 1284), Nant Eglos (OC), '*church valley*'

Lanteglos By Camelford (*Nanseglos* 1311), Nans Eglos, '*church valley*'

Lantewey (*Nandywy* 1284), Nant Duwy (OC), '*valley of the Dewey river*'

Lantivet (*Namtiuat* 1086), Nant Tyvet (OC), '*cultivated valley*'

Lantyan (*Nantyan* 1296), Nant Yeyn (OC), '*cold valley*'

Lanyon (Gwinear) (*Coswin Wolward* C16), Coswynn Wolward, '*white wood* (+ ?)'

Lanyon (Madron) (*Lynyeyn* 1326), Lynyeyn, '*cold pool*'

Larrick (Lezant) (*Lanrek* 1284), Lannergh, '*clearing*'

Larrick (S. Petherwin) (*Lanrek* 1327), Lannergh, '*clearing*'

Latchley (OE, **læcc léah*), Latchlea, '*clearing by a boggy stream*'

Launcells (*Lanceles* 1204), Lanseles, '*Seled's church site*'

Launceston (*Lanstaventon* 1189), Lanstefan, '*St Stephen's church site* (+ OE *tún*)'

Lavethan (*Lavedewen* 1330), Nant Bedewen (OC), '*birch tree valley*'

Lawhippet (*Lawhybbet* 1592), Nant Wibed (OC), '*valley of gnats*'

Lawhitton (*Landwithan* 905), Nant Wydhen (OC), '*tree valley*'

Leaze (*Layes c.* 1580; OE, *lés*), Leas, '*pasture meadows*'

Leburnick, Nant Bronnek (OC), '*rush-grown valley*'

Leedstown (E, C19), Leeds Town, '*settlement built by Duke of Leeds*'

Leha or **Leah** (*Legha* 1318–1504), Legha, '*slab place*'

Lelant (*Lananta c.* 1150, *Ewny Lanante* 1522), Ewny Lananta, '*St. Euny at St Anta's church site*'

Lelant, Lower (*Tredraeth* 1339), Tredreth, '*strand farm*'

Lelizzick (*Lanwoledic* 1284), Lanwolesyk, '*Gwledic's church enclosure*'

Lerryn (*Leryon* 1284), Leryon, '*floods* (stream name)'

Lescudjack (*Lanscoisek* 1302), Nans Cojek, '*wooded valley*'

Lesingey (*Lyssungy* 1326), Lysungy, '*Iunci's court/ruin*'

45

Leskernick (*Leskernycke* 1568), Lyskernyk, *'ruin at a corner'*

Lesneage (*Lismanahec* 1150), Lysmanahek, *'administrative centre of Memeage'*

Lesnewth (*Lysnewyth* 1238), Lysnowyth, *'new court'*

Lesquite (Lanivet) (*Lostcoys* 1320), Lostcoos, *'tail of a wood'*

Lesquite (Pelynt), Lostcuit (OC), *'tail of a wood'*

Lestowder (*Lesteudar* c. 1400), Lysteudar, *'Teudar's court'*

Leswidden (*Leswyn* 1769), Lyswydn, *'white/fair ruin'*

Levalsa Meor (*Avalde* 1086), Avaljy Meur, *'great Avaljy ('apple-store')'*

Lewannick (*Lanwennoc* 1201), Lanwenek, *'Wenoc's church site'*

Lewarne (*Lanwern* 1184), Nant Wern (OC), *'alders valley'*

Lezant (*Lansant* c. 1125), Lansant (OC), *'holy (or Sant's) church site'*

Lezerea (*Lysgre* 1296), Lysgre, *'herd's ruin'*

Ley (OE, *léah*), Lea, *'clearing'*

Lidwell (*Lydewelle* 1357; OE, *hlýde wielle*), Lydwell, *'source of a noisy stream'*

Linkindale (*Lenkeyndeyrn* 1507), Lynkyndern, *'Cyndaern's pool'*

Linkinhorne (*Lankynhorn* 1269), Lankynhorn, *'Cynhoern's church site'*

Liskeard (*Lys Cerruyt* c. 1010, *Lyskyrrys* 1375), Lyskerwys, *'Kerwyd's/stag's court'*

Lithiack (*Leydek* 1394), Leydek (OC), *'muddy'*

Little Petherick (*Nansfenten* 1371), Nans Fenten, *'well/spring valley'*

Little Polgooth, Polgoodh Vian, *'little Polgooth'*

Lizard (Cor.? E.? F.? *Lesard* c. 1250), Lesard, ?*'lizard('s tail)'*

Lockengate (E, C18), Locking Gate, *'locking gate'*

Lodge Hill (*le Lodge* 1590), Lodge, *'lodge'*

London Apprentice (E, C19), London Apprentice, *(inn-sign, after a folk song)*

Longdowns (E, C19), Long Downs, *'long downs'*

Long Rock (E, C18), Long Rock, *'long rock'*

Longstone (St Ives) (E, C17), Longstone, *'standing stone'*

Longstone (St Mabyn) (E, C13), Longstone, *'standing stone'*

Looe, East (*Lo* 1237), Logh, *'deep-water estuary, ria'*

Looe, West (*Porthbighan* 1280, *Portbian* 1334), Porth Bian, *'little cove'*

Looe Mills (*Lomulle* 1327), Melyn Logh, *'mill on the Looe river'*

Lord's Waste (E), Lord's Waste, *'wasteland of the Lord of Cardinham'*

Lostwithiel (*Lostwythyel* 1349), Lostwydhyel, *'tail of a wooded area'*

Lower Bodinnar (*Bodinner Woles* 1300), Bo'dener Woles, *'lower Bosdener (Dener's dwelling')'*

Lower Clicker, Clegar Woles, *'lower Clegar ('crag')'*

Lowertown (Helston) (E, C19), Lower Town, *'lower settlement'*

Lowertown (Roche) (E, C18), Lower Town, *'lower settlement'*

Lower Woon (*Guoyn* 1335), Goon Woles, *'lower downs'*

Luckett (*Lovecott* 1557; OE, *Léofa cot*), Lovecot, *'Leofa's cottage'*

Ludgvan (*Lusuoneglos* 1366), Eglos Lujowen, *'church at a place of cinders'*

Ludgvan Leaze, Lyslujowen, *'manor of Ludgvan'*

Luxulyan (*Lansulyan* 1335), Lansulyan; Loksulyen, *'Sulgen's church site'*

Lydcott (*Lotkoyd* 1284), Lotcuit, (OC), *'grey wood'*

Lymsworthy (OE, *Lemmanhysworthy* 1327), Lemansworthy, *'Léofmann's holding'*

Lynstone (OE, *Lulleston* 1262), Lullaston, *'Lulla's farm'*

Mabe (*Lanvabe* n.d.), Lanvab, *'Mab's/son's church site'*

Mabe Burnthouse (E, *Burnt House* 1813), Burnt House, *'burnt house'*

Maders (*Metheros* 1325), Medhros, *'middle roughland'*

Madron (*Eglosmadern* 1394), Eglos Madern, *'St Madern's church'*

Maer (OE, *The Mere* 1584), Mere, *'pool'*

Magor, Magor, *'ruin'*

Maidenwell (OE, *mægden wielle*), Maidenwell, *'maiden's well'*

Maker (*Magre* 1428), Magor, *'ruin'*

Malpas (F), Malpas, *'bad crossing'*

Manaccan (*Managhan* 1395), Managhan, *'monk's place'*; (*Mynstre* 1283), Mynster, *'endowed church'*

Manaton (OE, *(ge)mænen tún*), Manenton, *'common farm'*

Manhay (*Menehye* 1668), Menehy, *'church land'*

Mankea (*Maenke* 1288), Men Ke, *'hedge stone'*

Marazanvose (*Marras an Voze* 1617), Marhas an Vos, *'market at the wall'*

Marazion (*Marghasbighan* 1359), Marhas Vian, *'little market'*; (*Marghasyou* 1331), Marhas Yow, *'Thursday market'*

Marhamchurch (*Marona c.* 1085), Marwyn, *'St Maerwyn'*

Markwell (E, *Aelmarches Wylle* 1018), Almarkwell, *'Aelmarch's well'*

Marshgate (E, C18), Marshgate, *'gate to a marsh'*

Marsland (OE, *Maddockeslonde* 1288), Madocsland, *'Madoc's land'*

Mawgan-in-Meneage (*Pluvogan* 1523), Pluw Vaugan, *'St Maugan's parish'*

Mawla (*Mola* 960), Moghla, *'pigs' place'*

Mawnan, Maunan, *'St Maunan'*

Mawnan Smith, Govel Vaunan, *'smithy at Mawnan'*

Maxworthy (OE, *Maccas worðig*), Maccasworthy, *'Macca's holding'*

Mayon (*Maen* 1284), Men, *'stone'*

Mean Toll, Men Toll, *'tax/tithe boundary stone'*

Meaver (*Mever* 1319), Mever, (?*meaning*)

Medlyn, Medhlyn, *'middle pool'*

Mehal Mill (*Melyn Myhall* 1474), Melyn Mihal, *'St Michael's mill'*

Melancoose (*Melyncoys* C14, *Mellangoose* C17) Melyn Goos, *'wood mill'*

Meledor (*Meinleder* 1201), Meyn Leder, *'slope stones'*

Melinsey, Melynjy, *'mill house'*

Mellangoose (Helston) (*Melyn Goys* 1535), Melyn Goos, *'woodland mill'*

Mellangoose (Wendron), Melyn Goos, *'woodland mill'*

Mellanvrane (*Melyn Bran* 1343), Melyn Vran, *'crow's/Bran's mill'*

Mellingey (Cubert), Melynjy, *'mill house'*

Mellingey (St Issey), Melynjy, *'mill house'*

Menabilly (*Mynnybelly, Mennebile* 1573), Men Ebelly, *'colts' stone'*

Menacuddle (*Menequidel* 1250), Mene'-cuidel (OC), '*hillside with a small wood*'

Menadarva (*Mertherderwa* 1285), Merther Derwa, '*grave of St Derwa*'

Menadue (Tintagel, St Cleer, Talland, St Breward), Mene' Du, '*dark hillside*'

Menadue (Luxulyan) (*Menethdu* 1279), Meneth Du, '*dark hillside*'

Menagissey (*Meny-utheck* 1256), Men Yudhek, '*Iudoc's stone*'; (*Milgysy* 1330), Milgyjy, '*hunting dog house*'

Menagwyns (*Meneythgwyens* 1385), Meneth Gwyns, Mene' Gwyns, '*wind(y) hillside*'

Mendennick (*Myndenack* 1546), Mindinek, '*fortified tip*'

Menear (*Menhyre* 1525), Menhir, '*standing stone*'

Menehay (*Menehy* 7832), Menehy, '*church land*'

Menerdue (*Menethdu* 1356), Meneth Du, '*black/dark hillside*'

Menheniot (*Mahynyet* 1311), Mahynyet, '*Hynyet's land*'

Menherion, Menhiryon, '*standing stones*'

Menna (*Meneth c.* 1510), Meneth, '*hill, hillside*'

Mennor (*Meneth* 1625), Meneth, '*hill, hillside*'

Menwinnion (*Menwynyon* 1303), Menwynyon, '*white stones*'

Meres (*Methros* 1386), Medhros, '*mid-roughland*'

Merrifield (OE, *myrgan feld*), Merry-field, '*pleasant open land*'

Merrose (*Methros c.* 1200), Medhros, '*mid-roughland*'

Merry Meeting (E, C17), Merry Meeting, '*pleasant meeting place*'

Merrymeet (E, C17), Merrymeet, '*pleasant meeting place*'

Merthen (*Merthyn* 1213), Merdhin, '*sea-fort*'

Merther (*Eglosmerther* 1201), Eglos Merther, '*church of a saint's grave*'

Merther Lane, Bownder Eglos Merther, '*lane to Merther*'

Mertheruny (*Merther Ewny* 1291), Merther Ewny, '*St Euny's grave/reliquary*'

Metherell (E, *Middylhille* 1327), Middle Hill, '*middle hill*'

Methleigh (*Medle* 1265), Medhle, '*middle place*'

Methrose (St Blazey), (*Methros* 1277), Medhros, '*middle hillspur*'

Methrose (Goran) (*Metheros* 1482), Medhros, '*middle hillspur*'

Mevagissey (*Lannvorech* 1230), Lanvorek, '*St Morec's church site*'

Michaelstow (*S. Michael of Hellesbiri* 1279), Henlys Mihal, '*St Michael's Helsbury*'

Middlehill (E), Middle Hill, '*middle hill*'

Middlewood (E), Middle Wood, '*middle wood*'

Millbrook (OE, *mylen bróc*), Millbrook, '*mill brook*'

Millcombe (*Plenentmylle* 1390), Melyn Pluwnenyd, '*Pelynt mill*'

Millendreath, Melyn Dreth, '*beach mill*'

Millewarne (*Maenlewern* 1289), Men Lewern, '*foxes' stone*'

Millook (*Mellek* 1349), Melek, '*honeyed (stream name)*'

Millpool (Germoe) (E, C19), Millpool, '*mill pool*'

Millpool (Cardinham) (E, C16), Mill-pool, '*mill pool*'

Milltown (Cardinham) (E, C16), Milltown, '*mill farm*'

Milltown (Lanlivery) (E, *Lambfordmylle* 1465), Lambford Mill, '*mill at Lambford*'

Mingoose (*Meyngoys* 1327), Meyn Goos, '*woodland stones*'

Minions (*Miniens* 1613), Mynyens, (*?meaning*)

Minster (*Mynster* 1296), Mynster, '*endowed church*'; (*Talcarn* 1483), Talcarn, '*brow-tor*'

Mitchell (OE, *Meideshol* 1239), Maidshole, '*maid's hollow*'

Mithian (*Midhyan* 1302), Mydhyan, (*?meaning*)

Mixtow (E, *Michaelstowe* 1502), Michaelstow, '*St Michael's holy place*'

Moditonham (OE, *Modytone* 1372), Mudditon, '*muddy farm*'

Molenick (*Melionach* 1309), Melyonek, '*clover patch*'

Molingey (*Mlyngy* 1302), Melynjy, '*mill house*'

Molinnis (*Molenys* 1502), Molenys, '*bare isolated place*'

Monkscross (E), Monk's Cross, '*Monk family's cross*'

Moorswater (E), Moors Water, '*marshes stream*'

Moresk (F, *Moreis c.* 1150), Morais, '*marsh*'

Mornick (*Morinicke* 1601), Moryonek, '*ant-infested*'

Morvah (*Morveth* 1327), Morvedh, '*sea grave*'

Morval (E, *Morwell* 1474), Moorwell, '*marsh well/stream*'

Morwenstow (S. *Morwinna* 1478), Morwenna, '*St Morwenna*'

Mount (Perranzabuloe) (E, C19), Mount, '*high place*'

Mount (Warleggan) (E, *Mount Pleasant* 1612), Mount Pleasant, '*pleasant high place*'

Mount Ambrose (E, C16), Mount Ambrose, '*James Ambrose's high place*'

Mount Charles (E, C18), Mount Charles, '*Charles Rashleigh's high place*'

Mount Hawke (E, C18), Mount Hawke, '*Hawke family's high place*'

Mount Hermon (E), Mount Hirven, '*high place near Hervan (longstone)*'

Mount Pleasant (E), Mount Pleasant, '*pleasant high place*'

Mountjoy (*Meyndy* 1284), Meyndy, '*house of stones*'

Mousehole (*Porthenys* 1310), Porth Enys, '*island cove*'

Muchlarnick (*Lanher* 1086), Lannergh, '*clearing*' (+ ME *moche*, '*great*')

Mudgeon (*Mogyon* 1385), M'ojyon, '*ox place*'

Mulfra (*Molvre* 1284), Molvre, '*bare hill*'

Mullion (*Eglosmeylyon* 1274), Eglos Melan, '*St Melan's church*'

Mulvra (*Molvre* 1370), Molvre, '*bare hill*'

Mylor (*Lanwythek* 1277), Lanwydhek, '*church site in a place of trees*'

Mylor Bridge (*Ponsnowythe* 1562), Ponsnowyth, '*new bridge*'

Nampara, Nans Para, '*bread valley*'

Nancarrow (*Nanskarow* 1476), Nans Carow, '*stag's valley*'

Nancassick (*Nanscasek* 1416), Nans Casek, '*mare's valley*'

Nanceddan (*Nansredden* 1658), Nans Reden, '*bracken valley*'

Nancegollan (*Nannsygollen* 1356), Nans Igolen, '*whetstone valley*'

Nancekuke (*Nancoig* c. 1170), Nans Coog, '*empty/worthless valley*'

Nancemabyn (*Namabon* c. 1470), Nans Mabon, '*Mabon's valley*'

Nancemellin (*Nansmelyn* 1317), Nans Melyn, '*mill valley*'

Nancemerrin (*Nansmerion* 1338), Nans Meryon, '*Merion's valley*'

Nancenoy (*Nansnoy* 1684), Nans Noy, '*Noy's valley*'

Nancherrow (*Nansserou* 1400), Nans Erow, '*acre valley*'

Nancledra (*Nanscludry* 1324), Nans Clodry, '*Clotri's valley*'

Nanjizel (*Nansusal* 1302), Nans Usel, '*howling valley*'

Nanjulian (*Nanselyn* c. 1510), Nans Elyn, '*elbow-shaped (stream name) valley*'

Nankelly (*Nanskelly* 1330), Nans Kelly, '*grove valley*'

Nankervis (*Nanskerwes* 1284), Nans Kerwys, '*stags' valley*'

Nanpean (*Nanspyan* 1380), Nans Pian, '*little valley*'

Nanphysick (*Nansfusik* 1359), Nans Fusik, '*happy/fortunate valley*'

Nanplough (*Nansblogh* 1334), Nans Blogh, '*bare valley*'

Nanquidno (*Nansgwynyou* 1327), Nans Gwynyow, '*Gwynyou's valley*'

Nansalsa (*Nansalwester* 1284), Nans Salvester, '*Sylvester's valley*'

Nansavallen, Nans Avalen, '*apple-tree valley*'

Nanscawen, Nans Scawen, '*elder tree valley*'

Nanseglos, Nans Eglos, '*church valley*'

Nansidwell (*Nansudwall* 1540), ?Nans Yudhal, '*Iudhael's valley*'

Nansladron, Nans Ladron, '*thieves' valley*'

Nansloe, Nans Logh, '*valley of Loe Pool*'

Nansough (*Nanshogh* c. 1350), Nans Hogh, '*pig's valley*'

Nanstallon (*Lantalan* 1201, Nanstalen 1392), Nans Alen, '*valley of the river Allen (Camel)*'

Nanswhyden (*Nanswethan* 1428), Nans Wydhen, '*tree valley*'

Nantithet (*Nanstedeth* 1535), Nans Tedeth, (?*meaning*)

Narkurs (E, *Knockers Hole* 1659), Knockers Hole, '*knackerman's hollow*'

Netherton (OE, *niðerra tún*), Netherton, '*lower farm*'

New Mills (Ladock) (*Melynewyth* 1364), Melyn Nowyth, '*new mill*'

Newbridge (Sancreed) (*Hallentacken* C19), Hal an Tegen, '*marsh on the river Tegen (pretty one)*'

Newbridge (Kenwyn) (E, C19), Newbridge, '*new bridge*'

Newbridge (Callington) (E), Newbridge, '*new bridge*'

Newford (Scilly) (E, *Newfort* 1650), Newfort, '*new fort*'

Newham (Truro) (OE, *níwe hám*), Newham, '*new homestead*'

Newham (Sithney) (OE), Newham, '*new homestead*'

Newlyn (*Lulyn* 1290–1368), Lulyn, '*fleet-pool*'

Newlyn East (*Eglosnyulyn* 1415), Eglos Nywlyn, '*St Nyulina's church*'

Newmill (Madron) (*Chynoey* 1831), Chynoy, '*Noy's house*'

Newmill (Kenwyn) (*Melynneweth* 1366), Melyn Nowyth, *'new mill'*

Newquay (*Tewynplustri* 1308), Tewyn Plustry, ?*'at Towan'*

Newmills (Ladock) (*Melynewyth* 1364), Melyn Nowyth, *'new mill'*

Newton (Lanhydrock) (E), Newton, *'new farm'*

Newton (St Austell), Newton, *'new farm'*

Newton Ferrers (OE, *níwan tún*), Newton Ferrers, *'Ferrers family's* (C17) *new farm'*

Newtown (Germoe) (E, C19), Newton, *'new settlement'*

Newtown (Lewannick) (E, C16), Newtown, *'new settlement'*

Newtown St Martin (E, *Neweton* 1620), Newton, *'new farm'*

Ninnes (Madron) (*Enys* 1403), Enys, *'isolated'*

Ninnes (St Ives) (*Enys* 1305), Enys, *'isolated'*

Ninnes (St Mewan) (*Enys* 1305), Enys, *'isolated'*

Noongallas (*Goongallish* 1687), Goon Gales, *'difficult downs'*

North Corner (E), North Corner, *'north corner'*

North Country (E), North Country, *'north country'*

North Hill (Henle 1238) (OE, *héan léage*), Henlea, *'high clearing'*

North Tamerton (Tamerton 1179), Tamer, *'settlement on river Tamar'*

Northcott (OE, *be norðen cot*), Northcot, *'north of the cottage'*

Notter (*Nodetorre c.* 1257; OE, *hnottan torr*), Nottan Tor, *'bare crag'*

Numphra (*Nomfra* 1589), an Woonvre, *'the hill downs'*

Okeltor (OE, *Tokelyng Torre* 1351), Oaken Tor, *'at the crag with an oak tree'*

Old Cardinham, Cardinan Goth, *'old Cardinham'*

Old Kea (*Landegei* 1184), Landege, *'thy St Kea's church enclosure'*

Old Park (E), Old Park, *'old paddock'*

Oldmill (E), Old Mill, *'old mill'*

Old Town (Scilly) (*Porthenor* C12), Porth Enor, *'cove of Ennor'*

Otterham (OE), Oteryham, *'river meadow by the river Ottery'*

Padderbury (*Padirdabury* 1364), Din Pedreda (OC), *'fort at Padreda'*

Padreda, Pedreda, *'four fords/watercourses'*

Padstow (*Lanwethenek* 1350), Lanwedhenek, *'St Guethenoc's church site'*

Pantersbridge (*Pontyesu* 1241), Pont Yesu (OC), *'Jesus bridge'*

Par (*Porth* 1327), Porth, Por', *'cove, harbour'*

Paramoor (*Pale Moore* 1659; ME, *pale more*), Pale Moor, *'marsh where pales are cut'*

Parc-an-growes, Park an Grows, *'the cross field'*

Parc-an-ithon, Park an Eythyn, *'the furze field'*

Parc-an-tidno (*Parkfyntynowe* 1419), Park Fentydnyow, *'springs field'*

Park Bottom (E), Park Bottom, *'lower end of Tehidy Park'*

Park Erissey, Park Erysy, *'Erisey family's field'*

Parkengear, Park an Ger, *'field of the fort'*

Parkengew, Park an Gew, *'field of the enclosure'*

Parkfield (E), Parkfield, *'paddock field'*

Patrieda, Pedreda (OC), *'four fords/ watercourses'*

Paul (Breweny 1284), Breweny, (?*meaning*)

Paul's Green (E, C18), *Paul's Green, 'Paul family's green'*

Pawton (Polltun 902, 980), Poll, *'pool'* (+ E. *tún, 'farm'*)

Paynter's Cross (E), Paynter's Cross, *'Paynter family's cross'*

Paynter's Lane End (E), Paynter's Lane End, *'end of Paynter's lane'*

Pednandrea, Pedn an Dre, *'top of the settlement'*

Pelyn (*Penlyn* 1296), Penlynn, *'head/end of a pool'*

Pelynt (*Plunent* 1086), Pluw Nenyd, *'St Nonnyd's parish'*

Penadlake (*Penhylek* 1394), Penhelyk, *'end/top of willows'*

Penair (*Penarth* 1650), Penardh, *'prominent hilltop'*

Penbeagle (*Penbegel* 1259), Penbegel, *'top of a hillock'*

Penberth (*Benberd* 932, *Penbyrhy* 1580), Benbryhy, *'foot of the Bryhy (dappled river)'*

Penberthy (*Penbyrghi* 1309), Penbryhy, *'head of the Bryhy (dappled river)'*

Pencalenick (*Penkelynnec* 1296), Penkelynek, *'end of a holly-grove'*

Pencarrow (Advent) (*Pencayrou* 1327), Penkerrow, *'end/top with forts'*

Pencarrow (Egloshayle) (*Pencarou* 1314), Pencarow, *'stag's top'*

Pencoise (Grampound), Pencoos, *'end/top of a wood'*

Pencoose (Cuby), Pencoos, *'end/top of a wood'*

Pencoose (Stithians) (*broncoys* 1278), Broncoos, *'hill wood'*

Pencoose (Truro), Pencoos, *'end/top of a wood'*

Pencoys, Pencoos, *'end/top of a wood'*

Pencrebar (OE, *Crewabere* 1284), Crowbeare, *'crows' grove'*

Pencuke (*Penkyuoc* 1311), Penkiogh, *'snipe's top'*

Pendarves (*Penderves* c. 1320), Penderves, *'end/top of an oak wood'*

Pendavey (*Penduwy* 1310), Penduwy, *'head of the river Dewey'*

Pendeen (*Higher Boscaswell* C19), Boscaswal Wartha, *'higher Boscaswell'*

Pendewey (*Bendewy* 1310), Benduwy, *'foot of the river Dewey'*

Pendine (*Pendyn* 1303), Pendin, *'head/principal fort'*

Pendoggett (*Pendewegoys* 1302), Pendewgos, *'end/top of two woods'*

Pendower (*Bondowar* 1558), Bendowr, *'foot of a stream'*

Pendrea, Pendre, *'prinicipal farm'*

Pendrift (*Pendref* 1318), Pendrev, *'principal farm'*

Pendrym (*Pendrum* 1237), Pendrumm, *'ridge top'*

Penelewey (*Penhalewey* 1308), Penhal Ewy, *'marsh end by the Ewy (yew river)'*

Penfound (*Penfoune* c. 1300), Penfowen, ?*'hilltop with a beech tree'*

Pengegon (*Pengygen* 1327), Pengegyn, *'end/top of a ridge'*

Pengelly (Breage), Pengelly, *'end/top of a grove'*

Pengelly (Crowan), Pengelly, *'end/top of a grove'*

Pengelly (St Ewe), Pengelly, *'end/top of a grove'*

Pengelly (St Teath), Pengelly, *'end/top of a grove'*

Pengersick, Pengersek, *'end of a reed marsh'*

Pengold (*Pengouel* 1302), Pengowel, *'end/top of an enclosed farm'*

Pengover Green (*Pengover* 1334), Pengover, *'end/top of a stream'*

Pengreep, Pengryb, *'end of a hillcrest'*

Pengrugla (*Pengregell* 1608), Pengrugel, *'hilltop with a small barrow'*

Pengwedna, Pengwedna, *'end/top of the Gwedna stream'*

Penhale (Madron), Penhal, *'end/top of a marsh'*

Penhale (Millbrook), Penhal, *'end/top of a marsh'*

Penhale (Mullion), Penhal, *'end/top of a marsh'*

Penhale (Perranzabuloe), Penhal, *'end/top of a marsh'*

Penhale (Ladock), Penhal, *'end/top of a marsh'*

Penhale (Tywardreath), Penhal, *'end/top of a marsh'*

Penhale-an-drea, Penhal an Dre, *'Penhale by the farm'*

Penhale Jakes, Penhal Jakys, *'Jakes's Penhale'*

Penhallick (Camborne) (*Penhelek* 1314), Penhelyk, *'end/top of willows'*

Penhallick ((St Keverne), Banadhlek, *'broom-brake'*

Penhallow (Perranzabuloe), Penhallow, *'end/top of marshes'*

Penhallym (*Penalun* 1244), Penalen, *'head of the Allen stream'*

Penhalurick (Stithians), Penhal Lurik, *'defended Penhale'*

Penhalvean (Stithians), Penhal Vian, *'little Penhale'*

Penhalveor (Stithians), Penhal Veur, *'great Penhale'*

Penhargard, Penhirgarth, *'end of a long ridge'*

Penhellick (Camborne) (*Penhelek* 1314), Penhelyk, *'hilltop with willows'*

Penhellick (St Wenn) (*Penehelek* 1327), Penhelyk, *'hilltop with willows'*

Penhesken, Penheskyn, *'end of sedge'*

Penjerrick (*Pennanseyryk* 1333), ?Pennans Eyryk, (*?meaning*)

Penkestle (*Penkastel c.* 1535), Pencastel, *'castle top'*

Penknight (*Penknegh* 1284), Penknegh, *'top of a hillock'*

Penmarth (*Pengarth* 1337), Pengarth, *'end/top of a ridge'*

Penmayne (*Penmayn* 1227), Penmeyn, *'end/top of stones'*

Penmenor (*Penmeneth* 1512), Penmeneth, *'end/top of a hillside'*

Penmount (late C19) (*Penhellek vyan* 1429), Penhelik Vian, *'little Penhellick'*

Pennance (Budock), Pennans, *'end/head of a valley'*

Pennance (Gwithian) (*Pennans* 1302), Pennans, *'end/head of a valley'*

Pennance (Redruth), Pennans, *'end/head of a valley'*

Pennance (Zennor), Pennans, *'end/head of a valley'*

Pennant (Blisland) (*Pennant* 1550), Pennant (OC), *'head of a valley'*

Pennant (Dobwalls) (*Pennant* 1357), Pennant (OC), *'head of a valley'*

Pennant (Lanlivery), Pennant (OC), *'head of a valley'*

Pennant (St Endellion) (*Pennant* 1428), Pennant (OC), *'head of a valley'*

Pennare (*Pennarth* 1332), Penardh, '*prominent headland*'

Pennatillie (*Penansdelyowe* 1618), Pennans Delyow, '*head of the Delyow (leaves) valley*'

Pennygillam (*Pennaguinuall* 1311), Penaj'ynnyal, '*end of a desolate gap*'

Pennytinney (*Penventenyou* 1349), Penventynnyow, '*spring-heads*'

Penolva (*Penwolva* 1352), Penwolva, '*lookout top*'

Penpell, Penpell, '*far end*'

Penpethy (*Tympethy* 1296, *Tynpeythi* 1426), Tynpeythy, (*?meaning*)

Penpillick (*Penpelic* 1302), Penpellyk, '*little Penpell*'

Penpol (Feock), Penpoll, '*head of a creek*'

Penpoll (Crantock), Penpoll, '*head of a creek*'

Penpoll (Mawnan), Penpoll, '*head of a creek*'

Penpoll (St Veep), Penpoll, '*head of a creek*'

Penponds (*Penpons* 1252), Penpons, '*end of a bridge*'

Penpont (St Breward) (*Penpons* C20), Penpons, '*end of a bridge*'

Penpont (Wadebridge), Penpont (OC), '*end of a bridge*'

Penquite (Golant) (*Penquyte c.* 1470), Pencuit (OC), '*end/top of a wood*'

Penquite (Landrake) (*Pencoet* 1286), Pencuit (OC), '*end/top of a wood*'

Penquite (St Breward), Pencuit (OC), '*end/top of a wood*'

Penrice (St Austell) (*Penres* 1262), Penres, '*head of a watercourse*'

Penrose (Breage), Penros, '*end/top of a hillspur*'

Penrose (Budock), Penros, '*end/top of a hillspur*'

Penrose (Luxulyan), Penros, '*end/top of a hillspur*'

Penrose (Sennen), Penros, '*end/head of a hillspur*'

Penrose (St Breward), Penros, '*end/head of a hillspur*'

Penrose (St Columb), Penros, '*end/head of a hillspur*'

Penrose (St Ervan), Penros, '*end/head of a hillspur*'

Penrose (Sithney) (*Penros Methle* 1367), Penros Medhle, '*end/head of a hillspur at Methleigh*'

Penryn, Penrynn, '*promontory*'

Pensagillas (*Pensugelis* 1525), Pensugalys, '*end/top of rye-growing land*'

Penscawn (*Penscawen* 1306), Penscawen, '*hilltop with an elder tree*'

Pensilva (*Pensilva* 1868), Pensylva, (*after Silver Down nearby*)

Penstrassoe, Penstrasow, '*head of flat-bottomed valleys*'

Penstraze (*Penstras* 1340), Penstras, '*end/head of a flat-bottomed valley*'

Pentevale (*Penfenton fala* 1320), Penfenten Fala, '*source of the river Fal*'

Pentewan (*Bentewyn* 1297), Bentewyn, '*foot of the stream called Tewyn ('radiance')*'

Pentire, Pentir, '*promontory*'

Pentireglaze, Pentir Glas, '*green Pentire*'

Pentreath, Pentreth, '*head of a beach*'

Penventinue (*Penfentenyou* 1284), Penventynnyow, '*spring-heads*'

Penventon (Carn Brea), Penventen, '*spring-head*'

Penventon (Gwennap), Penventen, '*spring-head*'

Penventon (Helston), Penventen, *'spring-head'*

Penvose (Penryn), Penvos, *'end of a wall/bank'*

Penvose (St Tudy), Penvos, *'end of a wall/bank'*

Penwarne (Mawnan), Penwern, *'end/top of alder trees'*

Penwarne (Mevagissey), Penwern, *'end/top of alder trees'*

Penwartha, Penwartha, *'higher end'*

Penweathers (*Penwothes* 1327), Penwodhys, *'head of a place of streams'*

Penwerris (*Penweres* 1285), Penweres, *'head of a slope'*

Penwithick (*Penwythek c.* 1550), Penwydhek, *'end/top of a place of trees'*

Penzance (*Pensans* 1204), Pensans, Penzans, *'holy/sacred headland'*

Percuil (*Porthcule* 1613), Porth Cul, *'narrow cove/harbour'*

Perdredda (*Pydrede* 1306), Pedreda (OC), *'four fords/watercourses'*

Perranarworthal (*Peran Arwothel* 1612), Peran ar Wodhel, *'St Peran facing watery ground'*

Perrancoombe (*Piran Coombe c.* 1810), Comm Peran, *'St Peran's valley'*

Perranporth (*Tywarnheil* 1303), Ty war'n Heyl, *'manor on the Heyl (tidal flats)'*

Perranuthnoe, Peran Uthno, *'St Peran in Uthno manor'*

Perranwell (Perranarworthal) (E, C17), Peran Well, *'St Peran's well'*

Perranwell (Perranzabuloe) (*Fenton Berran* 1680), Fenten Beran, *'St Piran's well'*

Perranzabuloe (*Peran treth c.* 1608), Peran Treth, *'St Piran's sand'*

Peruppa (F, *Beaurepair* 1313), Beaurepair, *'pleasant retreat'*

Peterville (E, C18), Peterville, *'Peter family's town (F. ville)'*

Petherwin, North (*North Piderwine* 1259), Padarnwynn Cledh, *'North (holy) St Padarn'*

Petherwin, South (*Pidrewyn c.* 1147), Padarnwynn, *'holy St Padarn'*

Phillack (*Eglasheil* C12), Eglos Heyl, *'church on the tidal flats'*

Philleigh (*Eglosros* 1311), Eglos Ros, *'church of Roseland'*

Piece (E, C19), Picce, *'small plot of land'*

Pill, Pyll, *'creek' (adopted from ME)*

Pillaton (*Pilatone* 1086; OE, *píla tún*), Pilaton, *'farm defended by stakes'*

Piper's Pool (E, C16), Piper's Pool, *'Piper family's pool'*

Pits Mingle, Pyttys Mengleudh, *'quarry pits'*

Pityme (E, C18), Pity Me, *'(nickname) poor dwelling/land'*

Place (Fowey), Plas, *'mansion'*

Place (St Anthony in Roseland), Plas, *'mansion'*

Plaidy (*Playdy* 1823), Playdy, *(?meaning)*

Plain Street (E, C18), Plain Street, *'level road'*

Plain-an-gwarry (Marazion), Plen an Gwary, *'amphitheatre'*

Plain-an-gwarry (Redruth), Plen an Gwary, *'amphitheatre'*

Plashford (OE, *plæsc ford*), Pleshford, *'marshy ford'*

Playing Place (E, *Kea Playing Place* 1813), Kea Playing Place, *'amphitheatre at Kea'*

Pleming (*Plemmen* 1386), ?Plumen, *'plum tree'*

Plusha (*Plysshe* 1428; OE, *plæsc*), Plysh, '*marshy place*'

Plushabridge (E), Plysh Bridge, '*bridge at Plusha*'

Point (Feock) (E, *Daniell's Point* 1866), Daniell's Point, '*Daniell family's headland*'

Polapit Tamar (OE, *Bulapit* 1149), Bullapit Tamer, '*bullpit near the Tamar river*'

Polbathic (*Polbarthek* 1365, *Polvathick* 1748), Polbarthek, (?*meaning*)

Polborder (*Polbother* 1200), Polbodhowr, '*dirty-water pool*'

Polbrock (*Polbrogh* 1321), Polbrogh, '*badger's pool*'

Polcrebo (*Polcrybou* 1380), Polcrybow, '*pool by crests / ridges*'

Poldew (*Poldu* 1446), Poldu, '*dark pool*'

Poldowrian (*Bendowrian* 1250), Bendowran, '*foot of a watering place*'

Poldrissick (*Poldrysoc* 1275), Poldreysek, '*brambly pool*'

Poleo (*Polleowe* 1483), Pollew, '*pool by yew trees*'

Poley's Bridge (E, C16), Pawley's Bridge, '*Pawley family's bridge*'

Polgassick (*Polgasick* 1841), Polgasek, '*mare's pool*'

Polgear (*Polker* 1349), Polker, '*pool by a fort*'

Polgigga (*Pensiger* 1327), Pensiger, '*head of the Siger (stream name)*'

Polglase (Crowan), Polglas, '*green / blue pool*'

Polglase (Cury), Polglas, '*green / blue pool*'

Polglase (Wendron), Polglas, '*green / blue pool*'

Polglaze (Fowey) (*Polglas* 1386), Polglas, '*green / blue pool*'

Polglaze (St Austell) (*Polglas* 1296), Polglas, '*green / blue pool*'

Polglaze (St Mabyn), Polglas, '*green / blue pool*'

Polgooth (*Polgoyth* 1500), Polgoodh, '*goose pool*'

Polhigey, Polheyjy, '*ducks' pool*'

Polkanuggo, Polcronogow, '*frogs' / toads' pool*'

Polkerris (*Polkerys* 1585), Polkerys, '*fortified pool*'

Polkerth, Polkerhydh, '*heron's pool*'

Polkinghorne (Gwinear), Polkenhorn, '*Cynhoern's pool*'

Polkinghorne (Madron), Polkenhorn, '*Cynhoern's pool*'

Polladras, Polladres, '*sluice-gate pool*'

Pollawyn (*Penhalwyn* 1302), Penhal Wynn, '*white Penhal (marsh-end)*'

Polmanter (*Porthmanter* 1298), Porthmentir, '*gateway to Mentir (stone-land)*'

Polmarth, Polmargh, '*horse pool*'

Polmassick (*Ponsmadek* 1301), Ponsmasek, '*Madoc's bridge*'

Polmear (*Porthmuer* 1403), Porth Meur, '*large cove*'

Polmenna (Dobwalls) (*Polmena* 1627), Pollmene', '*hillside pool*'

Polmenna (St Neot) (*Penmeneth* 1532), Penmeneth, Penmene', '*hill top*'

Polmenna (St Winnow) (*Penmene* 1196–1356), Penmeneth, Penmene', '*hill top*'

Polmorla (*Polmorva* 1208), Polmorva, '*marsh pool*'

Polpeor (Lelant), Polpur, '*clean pool*'

Polpenwith (*Penreth* 1483, *Polpenruth* 1506), Penrudh; Poll Penrudh, '(*creek at*) *red top/end*'

Polperro (*Porthpera* 1355), Porth Pera, '*Pera's cove/harbour*'

Polridmouth (*Porthredeman* 1443), Porth Rydmen, '*stone-ford cove*'

Polruan (*Porthruan* 1284, *Polruen* 1371), Porth Reun, '*seal cove*'

Polrudden (*Polreden* 1321), Polreden, '*bracken pool*'

Polscoe (Fowey) (*Polkoth* 1314), Polcoth, '*old pool*'

Polscoe (St Winnow) (*Polescat* 1086, *Polscoth* C13) Polscath, '*boat pool*'

Polstain (*Polstene* 1522), Polsten, '*tin-pit*'

Polstangey Bridge (*Ponstangey* 1690), Pons Tangy, '*Tangye's bridge*'

Polstreath, Polstredh, '*stream pool*'

Polstrong (*Polstronk* 1302), Polstronk, '*filthy pool*'

Polsue (Philleigh) (*Bossue* 1538), Bosdu, '*black/dark dwelling*'

Polsue (St Clement), Poldu, '*black/dark pool*'

Poltarrow (*Poltarow* 1327), Poltarow, '*bull's pool*'

Poltesco (*Poltuska* 1380), Poltusca, '*moss pool*'

Polurrian (*Boloryan* 1580), Beleryon, '*cress beds*'

Polveithan (*Penvuthyn* 1330), Penvudhyn, '*end/top of a meadow*'

Polventon (*Penfenten* 1435), Penventen, '*springhead*'

Polwhele (*Polwhyl* 1350), Pollwhil, '*pool of beetles*'

Polwhevral (*Polwhefrer* 1298), Polwhevrer, '*lively pool/creek*'

Polyphant (*Polefant* c. 1170), Pollefant (OC), '*toad pool*'

Polzeath (*Polsegh* 1311), Polsegh, '*dry pool*'

Poniou (*Ponjou* c. 1841), Ponjow, '*bridges*'

Ponjeverah (*Ponsaravith* 1591), Pons Aravyth, (?*meaning*)

Ponjou, Ponjow, '*bridges*'

Ponsandane, Pons Anden, '*Endean's bridge*'

Ponsanooth (*Ponsanwoth* 1613), Pons an Wooth, '*bridge at the stream*'

Ponsharden (*Ponshardy* 1677), Pons Hardy, '*Hardy's bridge*'

Ponsmedda (*Ponsmerther* 1325), Pons Merther, '*bridge at Ruan Minor*'

Ponsmere (*Pons* 1338), Pons; Pons Meur, '*bridge*; *great bridge*'

Ponsongath, Pons an Gath, '*the cat's bridge*'

Ponsonjoppa, Pons an Shoppa, '*bridge at the workshop*'

Ponsontuel, Pons an Tewel, '*bridge at the conduit*'

Pont, Pont (OC), '*bridge*'

Pontshallow, Pons Hallow, '*marshes bridge*'

Pool (E, C18), Pool, '*pool*'

Pool (Scilly) (OE, *Sturtom* 1652, *steort hám*), Stertham, '*promontory homestead*'

Porcupine (E), Porcupine Inn, (*after a public house*)

Porkellis (*Porthkelles* 1286), Porth Kelys, '*gate to a hidden place*'

Port Eliot (E, C16), Port Ellyot, '*port of the Ellyot family*'

Port Gaverne (*Portkaveran* 1343), Porth Gavryn, ('*cove at the stream called Gavryn*')

Portgiskey (*Port Kiskey* 1794), Porth Kysky, (?*meaning*)

Porth (St Columb Minor) (*Porthmur* 1284), Porth Meur, '*large cove*'

Porthallack, ?Porth Helyk, '*willows cove*'

Porthallow (St Keverne) (*Porthalaw* 967), Porth Alow, '*cove of the Alow (water-lily stream)*'

Porthallow (Talland) (*Portallen* 1201), Porth Tallan, '*Talland cove*'

Porthcollum (*Polkellom* 1317), Pol-kellom, '*shelterless pool*'

Porthcothan (*Portgohedon c.* 1250), Porth Gohedhen, '*cove by a small barley plot*'

Porthcurno (*Porth Cornowe* 1580), Porth Cornow, '*cove of horns, pinnacles*'

Porthgwarra (*Porthgorwethau* 1387), Porth Gorwedhow, '*cove of wooded slopes*'

Porthgwidden (Feock) (*Porthgwyn* 1284), Porth Gwydn, '*white/fair cove*'

Porthgwidden (St Ives) (*Porthe Gwyne* 1580), Porth Gwydn, '*white/fair cove*'

Porthilly (*Porthylly* 1541), Porth Hyly, '*saltwater cove*'

Porthkea, Porth Ke, '*gate to Kea*'

Porthkerris (*Porthkersis* 1291), Porth Kersys, '*reedy cove*'

Porthleven, Porth Leven, '*cove of the river Leven ('smooth')*'

Porthluney, Porth Leveny, '*cove at the Luney river*'

Porthmeor, Porth Meur, '*large cove*'

Porth Navas (*Porranavas* 1649), Porth an Navas, (*?meaning*)

Portholland (*Portalan* 1288), Porth Alen, '*cove of the river Alen (Camel)*'

Porthoustock (*Portheustek* 1360), Porth Ewstek, '*Eustoc's cove*'

Porthpean (*Porthbyhan* 1297), Porth Bian, '*little cove*'

Porthtowan, Porth Tewyn, '*cove of Towan manor*'

Port Isaac (*Porthissek c.* 1540), Porth Ysek, '*corn-rich cove*'

Portloe, Porth Logh, '*deep water cove*'

Portlooe (*Porthlo* 1302), Porth Logh, '*gateway to Looe*'

Portmellon (*Porthmelyn* 1539), Porth Melyn, '*mill cove*'

Portquin (*Porthguyn* 1297), Porth Gwynn, '*white/fair cove*'

Portreath, Por' Treth, '*sand cove*'

Portscatho, Porth Scathow, '*boats cove/harbour*'

Portwrinkle (*Port Wrickel* 1605), Porth Wikel, '*cove at a small forest settlement*'

Poughill (*Pochewelle* 1227; OE, *pohha wielle*), Poghwell, '*stream with a fish-trap*'

Poundstock (OE, *pund stoc*), Pound-stock, '*settlement with a pound*'

Praze, Pras, '*meadow*'

Praze-an-beeble, Pras an Bibel, '*meadow of the conduit*'

Predannack (*Predennek* 1284), Preden-nek, '*British (headland)*'

Presingoll (*Presencoll* 1461), Prys an Goll, '*the hazel-trees grove*'

Pridden (*Penryn* 1363), Penrydn, '*hill-spur*'

Prideaux (St Blazey) (*Pridias c.* 1180–1346), Prydyes (OC), ?'*copses*'

Probus (*Lanbrobes* 1302), Lanbrobes, '*St Probus's church site*'

Prospidnick (*Pryspinik* 1284), Prys-pinek, '*pine copse*'

Pulla Cross, Crowshyns Pollow, '*pools*'

Pulsack (*Polsulsek* 1334), Polsolsek, '*profitable pool*'

Quarle (ME, F, *atte Quarrere* 1337), Quarry, '*at the quarry*'

Quenchwell (E), Quench Well, *'thirst-quenching well'*

Quethiock (*Quedoc* 1201), Cuidek (OC), *'wooded'*

Quillets (E), Quillets, *'small paddocks'*

Quintrell Downs (E, C12), Quinterell 1539), Coyntrel, *'Coyntrel family'*

Quoit (*Coyt* 1450), Coyt, *'dolmen'*

Race (*Reys* 1473), Res, *'watercourse'*

Radnor (E), Radnor, (*after Earls of Radford [Robartes]*)

Raftra (*Raghtre* 1302), Ragtre, *'facing a farm'*

Raginnis (*Ragenys* 1340), Ragenys, *'facing an island'*

Rame (Wendron) (E, C17), Rame, *'Rame family'*

Rame (Maker with Rame) (*Rama* 1086; OE, **hrama*), Rama, *'(place at) a barrier'*

Raphael (Resfrawel 1284), Resfrawel, (*?meaning*)

Readymoney (Mundy 1811), Mondy, *'mineral house'*

Reawla (*Realu* 1342; MF, *reial leu*), Reial Lieu, *'royal place'*

Receven (Resseuen 1481), Resewen, *'yew ford'*

Redevallen (*Redevallan* 1306, *Rosavallen* 1359) Resavalen, *'apple-tree ford'*

Redgate (E, C18), Redgate, *'red gate'*

Redinnick, Redenek, *'fern-brake'*

Redmoor (*Redemor* 1301; OE, *hréod mór*), Reedmoor, *'reed marsh'*

Redpost (*Redderise c.* 1170), Rederes (OC), *'ploughland ford'*

Redruth (*Unyredreth* 1563), Ewny Redrudh (OC), *'St Euny at a red ford'*

Redtye (E, C18 dialect), Red Tye, *'red trough (mining term)'*

Reen (*Run* 1338), Run, *'hill, slope'*

Rejarne (*Rosenhoern* 1317), Rosyn Horn, *'Hoern's (or iron) little hillspur'*

Rejerrah (*Rosworou* 1327, *Resorrow* 1630), Resworow, *'Gorou's ford'*

Releath (*Redlegh* 1270), Re'legh, *'slab ford'*

Relistian (*Rysclystyn* 1342), Rysclystyn, (*?meaning*)

Relubbus (*Reslehoubes c.* 1250), Res-lehoubes, *'Lehoubes's ford'*

Reperry Cross (*Respery* 1300), Respery, *'kite's ford'*

Rescassa (*Roscada* 1269, *Roscasa* 1390), Roscasa, *'Cada's hillspur'*

Rescorla (St Ewe), Roscorlan, *'hillspur with a stock pen'*

Rescorla (Stenalees) (*Roscorle* 1360), Roscorle, (*?meaning*)

Reskadinnick (*Roscadethek* 1284), Roscadedhek, *'Cadedoc's roughland'*

Reskajeage (*Roskadaek* 1317, *Rescasek* 1447), Roscajek, *'Cadoc's roughland'*

Resparva (*Rosperveth* 1341), Ros-perveth, *'middle hillspur'*

Respryn (*Ridpryne* 1270), Rysprenn, *'timber ford'*

Restormel (*Rostormel* 1175), Ros-tormol, *'hillspur at a bare eminence'*

Restowrack (*Rosdowrack* 1357), Ros-dowrek, *'watery roughland'*

Restronguet (*Rostronges* 1346), Ros-trongos, *'nose-wood promontory'*

Resugga (St Austell) (*Rosogou* 1317), Rosogow, *'hillspur with a cave'*

Resugga (St Stephen) (*Rosogou* 1304), Rosogow, *'hillspur with a cave'*

Resurrance (*Resgerens* 1321), Res-gerens, *'Gerent's ford'*

Retallack (Constantine) (*Reystalek* 1390), Restalek, *'watercourse with roach'*

Retallack (St Hilary) (*Restalek* 1311), Restalek, '*roach ford*'

Retallack (St Wenn) (*Reshelec* C13), Res'helyk, '*ford by willow trees*'

Retallick (Roche) (*Retelek* 1304, *Restelek* 1370) Res'helyk, '*ford by willow trees*'

Retanna (*Retanow* 1327), Re'tanow, '*thin/narrow ford*'

Retew (*Retteu* 1320), ?Retdu (OC), ?'*dark ford*'

Retire (*Redhyr* 1284, *Restyr* 1302), Res'hir, '*long ford*'

Retyn (*Restyn* 1334), Restin, '*ford by a rounded hill*'

Rezare (*Rescer* 1309), Resker, '*ford by a fort*'

Rialton (*Ryalton* 1283), Ryal, '*royal, regal*' (+ OE *tún*)

Rilla Mill, Melyn Ryslegh, '*mill at Rillaton*'

Rillaton (*Rislestone* 1086, *Ridlehtune c.* 1150), Ryslegh, '*slab ford* (+ OE *tún*)'

Rinsey (*Rynsy* 1390), Rynjy, '*promontory house*'

Rinsey Croft, Croft Rynjy, '*enclosed rough grazing at Rinsey*'

Rissick (*Resegh* 1312), Ressegh, '*dry ford*'

Roche (F, *La Roche* 1201), Roche, '*rock*'

Rock (*Penmayn* 1303), Penmeyn, '*end of stones*'

Rockhead (E, C18), Rockhead, '*ridge-end with a rock*'

Roscarnon, Roscarnen, '*roughland with a small cairn*'

Roscarrack (Budock) (*Rescadok* 1286), Rescadek (OC), '*Cadoc's ford*'

Roscarrock (St Endellion), Roscarrek Muer, '*great Roscarrock (rock roughland)*'

Roscroggan (*Roscrogan c.* 1200), Roscrogen, '*shell/skull roughland*'

Roscrowgey, Roscrowjy, '*uncultivated valley with a hut*'

Rose, Ros, '*roughland*'

Rose-an-growse (*Reysangrous* 1520), Res an Grows, '*watercourse at the cross*'

Rosecadghill (*Roscaswal* 1316), Roscajwal, '*Cadwal's roughland*'

Rosecare (*Roschel* 1086, *Resker* 1306), Rosker, '*hillspur with a fort*'

Rosecliston (*Reskylistyn* 1334), ?Reskellestryn, ?'*pebble ford*'

Rosecraddock (*Rescaradec* 1249), Ryscaradek (OC), '*Caradoc's ford*'

Rosedinnick (*Rosidenoch* 1208), Roseythynek, '*furzy hillspur*'

Rosehill (Altarnun) (E, *Rowehille* 1459), Row Hill, '*hill with a row (?of houses/ stones?)*'

Roseladdon (*Resledan* 1284), Resledan, '*wide ford*'

Roseland (Menheniot) (E, *Rowyslond* 1399), Rowesland, '*Rowe's holding*'

Roselyon (*Elyn* 1444, with modern addition), Elyn, '*elbow, bend (stream name)*'

Rosemanowas, Rosmenawes, '*awl-shaped hillspur*'

Rosemelling (*Rosemelyn* 1296), Rosmelyn, '*hillspur by a mill*'

Rosemellyn (*Resmelin* 1233), Resmelyn, '*mill ford*'

Rosemergy (*Rosmergi* 1356), Rosmerghjy, '*roughland with stables*'

Rosemerryn (*Rosmeren* 1414), Rosmeren, '*Meren's hillspur*'

Rosemodress, Rosmodres, '*Modret's roughland*'

Rosemorran (*Rosmoren* 1227), Rosmoren, '*Moren's hillspur*'

Rosemullion (*Rosmylyan* 1334), Rosmilyan, '*Milyan's promontory*'

Rosemundy (*Rosmundy* 1751), Rosmondy, '*roughland with an ore-house*'

Rosenannon (*Rosnonnen* 1326), Ros an Onnen, '*hillspur of the ash tree*'

Rosenithon (*Rosneython* 1249), Ros an Eythyn, '*roughland at the furze*'

Rosevallen (*Rosavallen* 1359), Rosavalen, '*apple-tree hillspur*'

Rosevath, Rosvargh, '*horse's roughland*'

Rosevean (*Rosvyan* 1327), Rosvian, '*little hillspur*'

Rosevear (*Rosveour* 1525), Rosveur, '*large hillspur*'

Rosevidney (*Rosevynny* 1306), Rosvydny, '*roughland with moorgrass*'

Rosevine (*Rosvreyn* 1302), Rosvreyn, '*putrid hillspur*'

Rosewall (*Ryswal* 1327), Ryswall, '*ford by a wall*'

Rosewarne (Gwinear), Roswern, '*roughland with alders*'

Rosewarne (Camborne) (*Risehoern* 1303), Reshorn, '*Hoern's ford*'

Rosewin (*Reswyn* 1450), Reswynn, '*white ford*'

Roseworthy (Gwinear) (*Reswori* 1289), Reswory, '*Gorhi's ford*'

Roseworthy (Kenwyn) (*Rosworgi* 1327), Rosworgy, '*Wurci's roughland*'

Roskear (Camborne) (*Resker* 1283), Resker, '*ford by a fort*'

Roskennals (*Resconwals* 1372), Resconwal, '*Cynwal's ford*'

Roskestal (*Roskastel* 1369), Roscastel, '*castle roughland*'

Roskilly, Roskelly, '*coastal slope with a grove*'

Roskorwell (*Roscurvyl c.* 1300), Roscurvyl, (*?meaning*)

Roskrow, Roscrow, '*roughland with a hut*'

Roskruge (*Roscruc* 1303), Roscrug, '*roughland with a barrow*'

Roskymer (*Reskemer c.* 1200), Reskemper, '*ford at a confluence*'

Rospannel, Rospanadhel, '*roughland with broom plants*'

Rospeath (*Rospygh* 1391), Rospigh, '*little hillspur*'

Rospletha (*Rosplethe* 1278), Rospleydh, '*wolf's roughland*'

Rosteague (*Rostek* 1400), Rosteg, '*beautiful promontory*'

Rosudgeon (*Rosusion* 1360), Rosujyon, '*roughland with chaff*'

Rosuick (*Rosewyk* 1327), Rosewyk, '*hind's roughland*'

Row (E, C19), Row, '*row (of houses)*'

Ruan High Lanes (E, *High Lanes* 1884), High Lanes, '*high lanes*'

Ruan Lanihorne (*Lanryhorn* 1270), Lanryhorn, '*Rihoern's church site*'

Ruan Major (*Merther* 1329), Merther, '*saint's grave*'

Ruan Minor (S. *Rumon in Woen* 1319), Rumon y'n Woon, '*St Rumon in the downs*'; (*Ruan Vean* 1569), Rumon Vian, '*little St Ruan*'

Ruddlemoor (OE, *Rydel* 1296), Rydel, (*?meaning*)

Rumford (OE *rúm ford*), Rumford, '*wide ford*'

Rushyford Gate (E), Rushyford Gate, '*gate at a rushy ford*'

Ruthdower, Rudhdowr, '*red stream*'

Ruthernbridge, Ponsrudhyn, '*bridge over the Ruthan river*'

Ruthvoes (*Ruthfos* 1296), Rudhfos, '*red wall*'

Ruzza (*Rosou* 1696), Rosow, '*hillspurs*'

Rytha (*atte Rytha* 1349; OE, *æt þæm ríða*), Ritha, '*at the streamlet*'

St Agnes (*Breanek* 1420–1499), Breanek, ?'*St Agnes's hill?*'

St Allen (*Eglosslan* 1235), Eglos Alun, '*St Alun's church*'

St Ann's Chapel (*Chapel of St Anna* 1500), Chapel Anna, '*St Anna's chapel*'

St Anthony in Meneage (*Lanyntenyn* 1344), Lanentenyn, '*St Antoninus's church site*'

St Anthony in Roseland (*S. Antoninus* 1170), Entenyn, '*St Antoninus*'

St Austell (*Austol c.* 1150), Austol, '*St Austol*'

St Blazey (*Landrayth* 1284), Landreth, '*church site at a beach/ferry*'

St Blazey Gate, Porth Landreth, '*gateway to St Blazey*'

St Breock (*Nanssant* 1381), Nans Sant, '*holy/Sant's valley*'

St Breward (*Brewered* 1327), Brewvered, '*St Brewvered*'

St Buryan (*Eglez Buryan c.* 1680), Eglos Beryan, '*St Beriana's church*'

St Cleer (*Clary* 1342, *Seint Cler* 1407), Sent Clar, '*St Clarus*'

St Clement (*Clemens* 1464), Clemens, '*St Clement*'

St Clether (*S. Cleder* 1259), Cledher, '*St Cleder*'

St Columb Major (*Plewgolom* 1543), Pluw Golom, '*parish of St Colom*'

St Columb Minor (*Colom* 1742), Colom, '*St Colom*'

St Columb Road, Fordh Golom, '*road to St Columb*'

St Day (*Seynt Dey* 1358), Sent Dey, '*St Dey*'

St Dennis, Dinas, '*hill fort*'; Din Mylyek, '*Milioc's fort*'

St Dominick (*Dominic* 1883), Domynek, '*St Dominica*'

St Elvan (*Seynt Helvan* 1270), Helvan, '*St Helvan*'

St Endellion (*Endelyn* 1522), Endelyn, '*St Endelienta*'

St Enoder (*Eglos Enoder* 1416), Eglos Enoder, '*St Enoder's church*'

St Enodoc (*Guinedouce* 1613), Gwenedek (OC), '*St Guenedoc*'

St Erme (*Egloserm* 1345), Eglos Erm, '*St Ermet's church*'

St Erney (*S. Ternin* 1434), Ternyn, '*St Ternin*'

St Erth (*Lanuthinoc* 1200), Lanudhynek, '*Guthinoc's church site*'

St Erth Praze (*Praze* 1748), Pras, '*meadow*'

St Ervan (*S. Ermete* 1208, *Ermet* 1327), Ermet (OC), '*St Ermet*'

St Eval (*S. Uvele* 1260), Uvel, '*St Uvel*'

St Ewe (*Lanewa* 1302), Lanewa, '*St Ewa's church site*'

St Gennys (*S. Guinas* 1086), Gwynas, '*St Guinas*'

St Germans (*Lannaled*, *Lanalet* C10), Lanaled, '*Aled's church site*'

St Gluvias (*Glewyas* 1565), Gluyas, '*St Gluviac*'

St Hilary (*Seynt Eler c.* 1680), Sent Eler, '*St Hilary of Poitiers*'

St Ingunger (*Stymgongar* 1283), Stumcongar, '*Congar's bend*'

St Issey (*Egloscruc c.* 1190), Eglos Crug, '*church on a barrow*'

St Ive (*S. Yvone* 1201, *S. Ivon* 1291–1327), Sent Ivon, '*St Ivon*'

St Ives (*Porthia* 1272–1695), Porth Ia, '*St Ia's cove/harbour*'

St Jidgey (*Sentysy* 1517), Yjy, '*St Ydi*'

St John (*Seynt Johan* 1372), Sent Jowan, '*St John*'

St Juliot (*Sanguilant* 1086), Gwylant, '*St Guilant*'

St Just in Penwith (*Lanuste* 1396), Lanust, '*St Just's church site*'

St Just in Roseland (*Lansyek* 1342), Lansiek, '*Sioc's church site*'

St Keverne (*Lannachebran* 1086), Lanahevran, '*Achebran's church site*'

St Kew (*Landoho* 1185), Landoho, '*Dochou's church site*'

St Kew Highway (E, *Highway* 1699), Highway, '*highway*'

St Keyne (*Cayne* 1342), Cayna, '*St Kayna*'

St Lawrence (*Seynt Laurens* 1380), Sent Laurens, '*St Lawrence*'

St Levan (*Sellevan* 1580), Selevan, '*St Selevan (Solomon)*'

St Loy (*Seynt Delow* 1400), Delow, '*St ?'Teilo*'

St Mabyn (*Sent Maban* 1327), Mabon, '*St Mabon*'

St Martin (Looe) (*Kayne the More* 1547), Caina Veur, '*great St Kayna*'

St Martin-in-Meneage (*Martyn* 1584), Martyn, '*St Martin*'; (*Dydemin* 1385), Dydemyn, '*St Dydemin*'

St Mawes (*Lavausa* 1445), Lanvausa', '*St Maudet's church site*'

St Mawgan (*S. Mauganus* 1260, *Mawgan* 1543), Maugan, '*St Maugan*'; (*Lanherno* 1257), Lanherno, '*Hernou's church site*'

St Mellion (*S. Melan* 1199, *Millians* 1553), Melan, '*St Melan*'

St Merryn (*Seynt Meryn* 1379, *Meren* 1584), Meryn, '*St Marina*'

St Mewan (*S. Mawanus* 1291, *Meuen* 1500), Mawan, '*St Mawan*'

St Michael Caerhays (*Lanvyhaill* 1473), Lanvihal, '*St Michael's church site*'

St Michael Penkevil (*Penkevel c.* 1210), Penkevyl, '*horse's head*'

St Minver (*Menfre* 1444), Menfre, '*St Menfre*'

St Neot (*S. Aniet* 1084), Anyet, '*St Aniet*'

St Pinnock (*Pynnoke* 1442), Pynnek, '*St Pynnoc*'

St Ruan (*Seyntrumon* 1382), Rumon, '*St Rumon*'

St Sampson, Sampson, '*St Sampson*'

St Stephen (Launceston), Lanstefan Coth, '*St Stephen's old church site*'

St Stephen-in-Brannel (*Egloshellans* 1379), Eglos Helans, '*Helant's church site*'

St Stephens, Sent Stefan, '*St Stephen*'

St Teath (*Egglostetha c.* 1190), Eglos Tetha, '*St Tetha's church*'

St Tudy (*Ecglostudic* 1086), Eglos Tudek, '*St Tudic's church*'

St Veep (*S. Vep* 1262), Vep, '*St Vepe*'

St Wenn (*S. Wenna* 1236), Wenna, '*St Wenna*'

St Winnow (*S. Wynnoc* 1331), Wynnek, '*St Winnoc* (?*Winwalo*)'

Saltash (*Essa c.* 1230, *Aysh* 1284; OE *æsc*), Ash/Essa, '*ash tree*'

Sancreed (*Eglossanres* 1440), Eglos Sancres, '*St Sancret's church*'

Sandplace (E), Sandplace, '*place where sand is stored*'

Sandylake (E, *Sandy Lakes* 1839), Sandy Lakes, '*sandy streams*'

Savath (*Enysvergh* 1423), Enysvergh, '*horses' isolated land*'

Saveock (*Sevyek* 1365), Seviek, '*strawberry land*'

Scarcewater (E, C18), Scarcewater, '*poor water supply*'

Scarrabine (*Roscarrec bian* 1249), Roscarrek Bian, '*little Roscarrack*'

Sclerder Abbey (Breton *sklaerder*), Abatty Clerder, '*abbey of clarity*'

Sconhoe (*Heskennow* 1302), Heskennow, '*sedges*'

Sconner (*Rosconeuer* 1311), Roskenvor, '*Cynvor's promontory*'

Scorrier (L, *Scorya* 1350), Scorya, '*mine waste*'

Scraesdon (*Creulisdon* 1349), Crewlys, '*weir by a ruin*'

Seaton (*Seythyn* 1302, *Sethon* 1578), Sethyn, '*little arrow (river name)*'

Seaureaugh or **Sewrah** (*Syuwragh* 1356), Syuwragh, (*?meaning*)

Sellan (*Seghlan* 1361), Seghlan, '*dry enclosure*'

Sellegan (*Reshelegen* 1291), Reshelygen, '*willow tree ford*'

Sennen (*Senan* 1480), Senan, '*St Senan*'

Sennen Cove (*Porth Gon Hollye* 1580), Porth Gonhyly, '*harbour serving Ganilly (Scilly)*'

Seworgan (*Reswothgan* 1528), Reswodhgen, '*Goethgen's ford*'

Sharptor (OE, *scearp torr*), Sharp Tor, '*sharp crag*'

Sheffield (E, *Sheffield Terrace* c. 1841), Sheffield Terrace, (*named from imported quarrymen*)

Sheviock (*Sevyok* 1284), Seviek, '*strawberry land*'

Shop (Morwenstow) (E, *Shop* 1840), Shop, '*workshop*'

Shop (St Merryn) (E, *Parkens Shop* 1748), Parken's Shop, '*Parken family's workshop*'

Shortacross (E, *Short Cross* 1732), Short Cross, '*short cross*'

Shortlanesend (*Penfounder* 1547), Penvownder, '*end of a lane*'

Shutta (*Shete* C12; OE, *scéota*), Shutta, '*place where trout are caught*'

Siblyback (E, C15), Sibilyback, '*Sibily family's ridge*'

Silena (*Sulghene* 1291, *Sulghenegh* 1321), ?Sulhenegh, (*?meaning*)

Sillaton (*Seleton* 1349; OE, *sele tún*), Seleton, '*farm with a hall*'

Silverwell (E, C18), Silver Well, '*silver well*'

Sinns (*Syns* 1456), Syns, '(*place of*) *holy men*'

Sithney (*Merthersythny* 1320), Merther Sydhny, '*St Sythni's grave*'

Sithney Common, Goon Sydhny, '*downs at Sithney*'

Skewes (Crowan) (*Skewys* 1334), Skewys, '*place of elder trees*'

Skewes (Cury) (*Skewys* 1326), Skewys, '*place of elder trees*'

Skewes (St Wenn) (*Skewys* 1409), Skewys, '*place of elder trees*'

Skewjack (*Skewyek* 1329), Skewjek, '*elder grove*'

Skinners Bottom (E, C18), Skynner's Bottom, '*Skynner family's valley bottom*'

Skyburriowe, Skiberyow, '*barns*'

Slades (OE, *slæd*), Slade, '*valley*'

Sladesbridge (*Layne Bridge* 1470), Pons Lain, '*bridge over the Layne river*'

Slaughter Bridge (E), Slaughter Bridge, *'slaughter bridge'*

Slipperhill (*Sleperhille* 1529; OE, *slypa hyll*), Slipahill, *'muddy slope'*

South Carne (*Suth Carn* 1314), Carn Soth, *'southern Carne'*

South Hill (*Suthhynle* 1306; OE, *súð héan léah*), South Henlea, *'southern Henlea (see* **North Hill***)'*

South Wheatley (E, *South Whitleigh* 1748), South Whitelea, *'southern Wheatley'*

Southcott (OE, *súð cot*), Southcot, *'southern cottage'*

Southdown (OE, *be súðan dúne*), Southdown, *'south of the hill'*

Spargo (*Spergor* 1208), Sperngor, *'thorn hedge'*

Sparnock (*Spernek* 1280), Spernek, *'thorny'*

Sparnon, Spernen, *'thorn tree'*

Sparnon Gate (*Spernen* 1327), Spernen, *'thorn tree'*

Splatt (St Minver), Splat, *'plot of land'*

Splatt (Tresmeer), Splat, *'plot of land'*

Splattenridden, Splat an Reden, *'the bracken plot'*

Stampas, Stampys, *'tin-stamping mill'*

Stannon (*Standon* C15; OE, *stán dún*), Standon, *'stone hill'*

Start (OE, *steort*), Stert, *'tongue of land'*

Stennack, Stenek, *'tinstream'*

Stenalees (*Stenaglease* 1621), Steneglys, *'manor's tinstream'*

Stencoose (St Agnes) (*Stumcoys* 1327), Stumcoos, *'bend of a wood'*

Stennack, Stenek, *'tinstream'*

Stepaside (E), Stepaside, *'narrow thoroughfare'*

Stephengelly (Lanivet) (*Stymguelli c.* 1300), Stumgelly, *'bend of a grove'*

Stephengelly (St Neot) (*Stymgelly* 1313), Stumgelly, *'bend of a grove'*

Stibb (OE, *stybb*), Stybb, *'tree stump'*

Sticker (*Stekyer* 1319), Stekyer, *'stumps'*

Stithians (*S. Stethyane* 1268, *Stythian* 1584), Stedhyan, *'St Stethyan'*

Stockadon (*Stocaton* 1321; OE, *stocca tún*), Stockaton, *'farm built from logs'*

Stoke Climsland (*Stok in Clymeslond* 1302), Stock in Clymsland, *'outlying farm in Clym's land'*

Stoketon (OE, *stocc tún*), Stockton, *'farm by a post'*

Stoptide (E, *Stop-a-tide* 1879), Stoptide, *'tidal limit'*

Stowe (OE *stów*), Stow, *'holy place'*

Stratton (*Strætneat c.* 880), Stradneth (OC), *'flat-bottomed valley of the Neth river'*

Street (OE, *strǽt*), Street, *'street'*

Street-an-nowan, Stret an Awon, *'street at the river'*

Strickstenton (*Tregestentyn* 1387), Tregostentyn, *'Constantine's farm'*

Stursdon (E, *Sturnelysdon* 1356), Sturnelsdon, *'Sturnell's hill'*

Suffree (*Resvreghy c.* 1500), Resvreghy, *'ford on the Breghy ('dappled') stream'*

Summercourt (E, *Longaferia* 1227), Longfair, *'long market'*

Summerleaze (OE, *sumor lǽs*), Summerleas, *'summer pasture'*

Sweets (E, *Sweets Tenement* n.d.), Sweet's Tenement, *'land held by the Sweet family'*

Sweetshouse (E), Swete's House, *'Swete family's house'*

Sworne (*Sowrne* 1571), Sorn, *'nook, corner'*

Talland (*Tallan* 1205), Tallan, *'hillbrow church site'*

Talskiddy (*Talskedy* 1300), Talskeudy (OC), '*shady hill-brow*'

Tamsquite (*Stymguyt* 1327), Stumguit (OC), '*bend of a wood*'

Taphouse, East (E, C17), East Taphouse, '*eastern alehouse*'

Taphouse, Middle (E, C17), Middle Taphouse, '*middle alehouse*'

Taphouse, West (*Taphouse* 1532), Taphouse, '*alehouse*'

Taskus (*Talscus* 1317), Talskeus, '*hill-brow giving shade*'

Tehidy (*Tihidin c.* 1120), Ty Hydyn, ?'*Hydin's manor*'

Temple (E), Temple, (*church founded by Knights Templar*)

Tencreek (Lansallos) (*Kyencruke* 1447), Keyncrug, '*ridge barrow*'

Tencreek (Menheniot) (*Trencruk* 1378), Tre'n Crug, '*farm at the barrow*'

Tencreek (St Veep) (*Trencruke* 1309), Tre'n Crug, '*farm at the barrow*'

Tenderra (*Tyndere* 1302), Tin Derow, '*rounded hill with oaks*'

Terras (*Terres* 1306), Teyr Res, '*three fords*'

Thankes (C14) *from the Thonkes family*; (*Pengelly* C13) Pengelly, '*end/top of a grove*'

Thorne (OE *þorn*), Thorn, '*thorn tree*'

Three Burrows (E, C18), Three Barrows, '*three barrows*'

Threemilestone (E, C19), Three Mile Stone, '*third milestone from Truro*'

Thurdon (*Thonnerdone* 1302; OE, *þunor dún*), Thunderdon, '*thunder hill*'

Thurlibeer (OE, *þyrel bearu*), Thurlbear, '*hollowed grove*'

Tideford (*Todiford* C13), Rystudy, '*ford on the Tiddy River*'

Tilland (*Tyllon* 1598; OE, *til land*), Tilland, '*useful land*'

Tintagel (village) (*Trewarvene* 1259), Tre war Vene', Tre war Veneth '*farm on a hillside*'

Tinten (*Tynten, Tynteyn* 1240), Tynten, (?*meaning*)

Tippet's Shop (E, C18), Teppet's Shop, '*Teppet family's workshop*'

Titson (*Tetyanston* 1313; OE) Tetyston, (?*meaning*)

Todpool (E, C19), Toadpool, '*toad's pool*'

Tolborough (*Tolburgh* 1417), Tolcrug, '*hollowed barrow*'

Tolcarne (Camborne), (*Talcarn* 1340), Talcarn, '*hill-brow tor*'

Tolcarne (Penzance), Talcarn, '*hill-brow tor*'

Tolcarne (St Columb Minor), Castel Talcarn, '*castle at a hill-brow tor*'

Tolcarne (Wendron) (*Talkarn* 1325), Talcarn, '*hill-brow tor*'

Tolgarrick (*Talgarrek* 1327), Talgarrek, '*brow rock*'

Tolgullow (*Talgolou* 1284), Talgolow, '*hill-brow of light*'

Tolgus (*Tolgoys* 1302), Tolgoos, '*hole-wood*'

Tolskithy (*Tolskethie* 1682, *Tolskithy* 1748), Tolskedhy, (?*meaning*); (*Rose-withan* 1655), Roswedhen, '*roughland with a tree*'

Tolvaddon (*Talvan c.* 1200), Talvadn, '*brow of a height*'

Tolvan, Tolven, '*holed stone*'

Tolver (*Talvargh* 1284), Talvargh, '*horse's/Meirch's hill-brow*'

Tolverne (*Talvron* 1275), Talvron, '*brow of a hill*'

Tonacombe (_Tunnecombe_ 1302; OE), Tunnacumb, '_valley of the Tunna stream_'

Torfrey (_Torfre_ 1284), Torvre, '_bulge hill_'

Torleven (_Treleven_ 1660), Treleven, '_farm on the river Leven_'

Torpoint (ME, _Stertpoynt_ 1608), Stert, '_tongue of land, promontory_'

Towan (St Agnes), Tewyn, '_stream called Tewyn ('radiance')_'

Towan (St Austell), Tewyn, '_stream called Tewyn ('radiance')_'

Towan (St Merryn), Tewyn, '_stream called Tewyn ('radiance')_'

Towanwroath, Toll an Wragh, '_the giant's hole_' (**wragh** '_hag_' _also means 'giant' in LC_)

Towednack (_Tewynnek_ 1524), Tewyd-nek, '_thy St Winnoc (Winwalo)_'

Townshend (E, C19), Townsend, '_Townsend family_'

Traboe (_Treuorabo_ 1284), Treworabo, '_Gorabo's farm_'

Trago (_Treiagu_ 1277), Treyago, '_Jacob's farm_'

Trannack (Madron) (_Trewethenec_ 1342), Trewedhenek, '_Guethenoc's farm_'

Trannack (St Erth) (_Trevranek_ 1325), Trevranek, '_Branoc's farm_'

Trannack (Sancreed) (_Trevranek_ 1302), Trevranek, '_Branoc's farm_'

Trannack (Sithney) (_Trewethenek_ 1406), Trewedhenek, '_Guethenoc's farm_'

Transingove (_Tanewancoys_ 1287), Tenewangoos, '_side-wood_'

Treamble (_Taranbol_ 1316), Taranbol, '_thunder pool_'

Treassowe (_Trevrasowe_ 1422), Tre-vrasow, '_Brasou's farm_'

Treath, Treth, '_ferry passage_'

Treator (_Tryetor_ 1327, _Treytard_ 1350), ?Tritard (OC), ?'_three rushing streams_'

Treave (St Buryan) (_Treyuff_ 1302), Treyuv, '_Yuf's farm_'

Treave (Sennen) (_Treyuf_ 1334), Treyuv, '_Yuf's farm_'

Trebah (_Treverybow_ 1316, _Trewribou_ 1329), Treverybow, (?_meaning_)

Trebarber (_Treberveth_ 1307), Tre-berveth, '_middle/inner farm_'

Trebartha (_Tribertham_ 1086), Tre-berthan, '_farm in a bushy place_'

Trebarvah (Perranuthnoe) (_Treberveth_ 1342), Treberveth, '_middle/inner farm_'

Trebarvah (Constantine), Treberveth, '_middle/inner farm_'

Trebarveth (St Keverne), Treberveth, '_middle/inner farm_'

Trebarveth (Stithians), Treberveth, '_middle/inner farm_'

Trebarwith (_Treberveth_ 1296), Tre-berveth, '_middle/inner farm_'

Trebeath (_Trebigh_ 1583), Trebigh, '_small farm_'

Trebehor (_Trebuer_ 1284), Trebuor', '_cow-yard farm_'

Trebell, Trebell, '_far farm_'

Trebetherick (_Trebedrek_ 1302), Tre-bedrek, '_Petroc's farm_'

Trebilcock (_Trebilcok_ 1380), Tre-bylcawgh, '_dung-heap farm_'

Trebisken (_Trebryskyn_ 1403), Tre-bryskyn, '_farm at a small copse_'

Trebowland (_Trebowlan_ 1391), Tre-bowlan, '_cow-pen farm_'

Trebrownbridge (_Trefron_ 1327), Tre-vronn, Pons Trevronn, '_hill farm_'

Trebudannon (_Trebydadnen_ 1575), Trebydadnen, '_Pydannen's farm_'

Trebullett (*Trebalvet* 1383), Trebalvet (OC), (*?meaning*)

Treburgett (*Trebridoc* C12, *Trebruthek* 1289), Trebrythek, '*farm in a dappled place*'

Treburley, Treborlay, '*Borlay family's farm*'

Treburrick (*Trebruthek* 1321), Trebruthek, (*?meaning*)

Trebursye (*Trebursi* 1199), Trebursy, '*Beorhtsige's farm*'

Trebyan (*Trebyghan* 1319), Trebian, '*small farm*'

Trecarne (Forrabury) (*Trecarne* 1338), Trecarn, '*tor farm*'

Trecarne (St Cleer) (*Talkarn* 1390), Talcarn, '*brow tor*'

Trecarne (St Teath) (*Talcarn* 1309), Talcarn, '*brow tor*'

Trecarrel (*Trecarl* 1202), Trecarl, ?'*Carl's farm*'

Trecrogo (*Trecrugow* 1397), Trecrugow, '*barrows farm*'

Tredannick (*Trethanek* 1360), Trethanek, '*Tanoc's farm*'

Tredarrup (Michaelstow) (*Tretharap* 1298), Trewortharap, '*very pleasant farm*'

Tredarrup (St Neot) (*Tretharap* 1401), Trewortharap, '*very pleasant farm*'

Tredarrup (St Winnow) (*Trethorop* 1476), Trewortharap, '*very pleasant farm*'

Tredarrup (Warbstow) (*Tretharap* 1411), Trewortharap, '*very pleasant farm*'

Tredaule (*Tredawel* 1302), Tredawel, '*quiet farm*'

Tredavoe (*Treworthavo* 1328), Treworthavo, '*Gorthavo's farm*'

Tredawargh (*Tredowargh* 1332), Tredowargh, '*turf farm*'

Tredeague (*Trethaeg* 1311), Tretheg, '*beautiful farm*'

Tredenham (*Tredynan* 1428), Tredinan, '*farm at a fort*'

Tredethy (*Tredetthe* 1420), Tredetha, '*St Tetha's farm*'

Tredinneck (Madron) (*Tredenek* 1457), Treredenek, '*fern-brake farm*'

Tredinnick (Duloe) (*Trethynek* 1302), Tredhinek, '*fortified farm*'

Tredinnick (Landrake) (*Tredinek* 1346), Tredhinek, '*fortified farm*'

Tredinnick (Lanhydrock) (*Tredenek* 1518), Treredenek, '*fern-brake farm*'

Tredinnick (Luxulyan) (*Tredenek* 1279), Treredenek, '*fern-brake farm*'

Tredinnick (Morval) (*Treveythynek* 1300), Trev Eythynek, '*furzy farm*'

Tredinnick (Newlyn East) (*Trethynicke c.* 1470), Tredhinek, '*fortified farm*'

Tredinnick (Probus) (*Treredenek* 1288), Treredenek, '*fern-brake farm*'

Tredinnick (St Issey) (*Treredenek* 1286), Treredenek, '*fern-brake farm*'

Tredinnick (St Keverne) (*Treredenek* 1311), Treredenek, '*fern-brake farm*'

Tredinnick (St Mabyn) (*Trethnyneke* 1421), Tredhinek, '*fortified farm*'

Tredinnick (St Neot) (*Trethynek* 1345), Tredhinek, '*fortified farm*'

Tredrea (*Tredrue* 1301, *Tredroe* 1363), Tredro, '*farm at a turning*'

Tredrizzick (*Trethreysek* 1284), Tredhreysek, '*brambly farm*'

Tredrossel (*Tredrysell c.* 1450), Tredreysel, '*bramble-place farm*'

Tredrustan (*Tredrystan* 1549), Tredrystan, '*Tristan's farm*'

Treen (St Levan) (*Trethyn* 1284), Tredhin, '*farm by a fort*'

Treen (Zennor) (*Trethyn* 1314), Tredhin, *'farm by a fort'*

Treesmill (Melyntrait 1150), Melyn Dreth, *'sand mill'*

Treffry (Lanhydrock) (*Trefry* 1356), Trefry, *'Fri's farm'*

Treffry (Merther) (*Trefry* 1320), Trefry, *'Fri's farm'*

Treforda (Camelford) (ME, *atte forde*), Atford, *'at the ford'*

Trefreock (*Trefryek* 1284, *Trevryek* 1324), Trevryck, *'Frioc's farm'*

Trefrew (*Trefrew* 1338), Trevrew, *'farm at a fragment of land'*

Trefrize (*Trevrys* 1300), Trevrys, *'ford farm'*

Trefronick (*Trevronek* 1334), Trevronnek, *'hilly farm'*

Trefula, Trev Ula, *'owl farm'*

Trefusis (*Trefusys* 1356), Trefusys, *?'well-utilized farm'*

Tregada (*Tregadou* 1321), Tregado, *'Cado's farm'*

Tregaddick (*Tregadek* 1305), Tregadek (OC), *'Cadoc's farm'*

Tregadgwith, Tregajwydh, *'thicket farm'*

Tregadillett (*Tregadylet* 1076), Tregadylet (OC), *'Cadylet's farm'*

Tregadjack (*Tregarasek* 1321), Tregarajek, *'Caradoc's farm'*

Tregair (*Tregaer* 1304), Treger, *'farm by a fort'*

Tregajorran (*Tregasworon* 1321), Tregajworon, *'Cadworon's farm'*

Tregamere (*Tregamur* 1422), Trigva Meur, *'great dwelling'*

Tregaminion (Morvah) (*Tregemynyon* 1327), Tregemynyon, *'commoners' farm'*

Tregaminion (Tywardreath) (*Tregeminyon* C16) Tregemynyon, *'commoners' farm'*

Treganhoe (*Tregenhogh* 1504), Tregenhogh, *'Cynhoch's farm'*

Tregantle (Antony) (*Argantel* 1086), Argantel (OC), *'silver stream'*

Tregantle (Lanlivery) (*Argantell* 1521), Argantel (OC), *'silver stream'*

Tregardock (*Tregaradoc* 1196), Tregaradek (OC), *'Caradoc's farm'*

Tregargus (*Tregargos* 1433), Tregargos, *'fort-wood farm'*

Tregarland (*Crugalein* 1166), Crug Alen, *'barrow on river Alen (Camel)'*

Tregarne (Mawnan), Tregarn, *'tor farm'*

Tregarne (St Keverne), Tregarn, *'tor farm'*

Tregarrick (Roche) (*Tregarrek* 1250), Tregarrek, *'rock farm'*

Tregarrick (St Cleer) (*Tregadek* 1440), Tregadek (OC), *'Cadoc's farm'*

Tregarthen (*Tregeuvran* 1262), Tregeuvran, *(?meaning)*

Tregassa, Tregasa, *'Cada's farm'*

Tregassick (Gerrans) (*Tregeroseke* 1454), Tregarasek, *'Caradoc's farm'*

Tregassick (Mevagissey) (*Tregadek* 1302), Tregasek, *'Cadoc's farm'*

Tregaswith, Tregaswydh, *'thicket farm'*

Tregatillian (*Tregentulyon* 1327), Treguntellyon, *'assemblies' farm'*

Tregatta (*Tregata* 1284), Tregata, *'Cata's farm'*

Tregatillian (*Trengentulyon* 1327), Tre'n Guntellyon, *'farm of the assemblies'*

Tregavarah (*Tregouvoro* 1316; *Govarrowe* 1628) Tregoverow, *'streams farm'*

Tregaverne (*Tregaveren* 1284), Tregavryn, *('farm by the Gavryn stream')*

Tregavethan (*Treganmedan* 1086), Tregenvedhan, '*Cynfedan's farm*'

Tregea (*Trege c.* 1250), Trege, '*hedge farm*'

Tregeagle (*Tregagel* 1241), Tregagal, '*dung farm*'

Tregear (Bodmin) (*Cayr* 1444), Ker, '*fort*'

Tregear (Crowan) (*Tregaer* 1318), Treger, '*farm by a fort*'

Tregear (Gerrans) (*Tregayr* 1249), Treger, '*farm by a fort*'

Tregear (Ladock) (*Tregaer* 1304), Treger, '*farm by a fort*'

Tregear (Mawgan) (*Tregaer* 1403), Treger, '*farm by a fort*'

Tregear (St Eval) (*Tregaer* 1256), Treger, '*farm by a fort*'

Tregeare (Egloskerry) (*Treger c.* 1150), Treger, '*farm by a fort*'

Tregeare (St Kew) (*Tregayr* 1416), Treger, '*farm by a fort*'

Tregellas (Probus) (*Tregellest* 1280), Tregelest, '*Celest's farm*'

Tregelles (St Kew) (*Tregelest* 1311), Tregelest, '*Celest's farm*'

Tregembo (*Trethygember* 1321), Tredhigemper, '*farm by a double confluence*'

Tregender (*Tregeneder* 1284), Tregeneder, '*Cynheder's farm*'

Tregenhorne, Tregenhorn, '*Cynhoern's farm*'

Tregenna (St Ives) (*Tregennowe* 1543), Tregenow, '*Ceneu's farm*'

Tregenver (*Tregenvor* 1590), Tregenvor, '*Cynvor's farm*'

Tregerest, Tregerest, '*Cerest's farm*'

Tregerrick (*Tregeryek* 1305), Tregeryek, '*Cerioc's farm*'

Tregerthen (*Tregyrthyn* 1519), Tregerdhyn, '*rowan tree farm*'

Tregeseal (*Tregathihael* 1248; *Tregathial* 1302), Tregathyel, '*Catihael's farm*'

Tregew (*Tregeu* 1208), Tregew, '*enclosure farm*'

Tregidden (*Tregudyn c.* 1190), Tregudyn, (*?meaning*)

Tregidgeo (*Tregrisyow* 1338), Tregryjyow, '*farm of folds / wrinkles (in landscape)*'

Tregiffian (St Buryan) (*Tregguhion* 1331), Treguhyon, '*wasp-infested farm*'

Tregiffian (St Just) (*Tregyffian* 1589), Tregyfyon, '*tree-stumps farm*'

Tregilliowe, Tregellyow, '*groves farm*'

Tregiskey (*Tregesky* 1284), Tregysky, (*?meaning*)

Treglennick (*Tregelennek* 1359), Tregelynek, '*holly-grove farm*'

Treglisson (Treglistyn 1326), Treglystyn, (*?meaning*)

Treglossick (Tregludek 1296), Treglosek, '*Clodoc's farm*'

Tregolds (*Tregatlos* 1277, *Tregathelos* 1327), Tregathlos, '*Catlod's farm*'

Tregole (*Tregewal* 1306), Tregewel, '*enclosed farm*'

Tregolls (*Tregollas* 1314), Tregollas, '*hazlett farm*'

Tregona (*Tregonou* 1327), Tregonow, '*Coneu's farm*'

Tregonce (*Tregendros* 1201), Tregendros, '*Cyndrod's farm*'

Tregonebris (*Tregenhebris* 1342), Tregenhebrys, '*Conhibrit's farm*'

Tregonetha (*Tregenhetha* 1341), Tregenhedha, '*Cynhedda's farm*'

Tregongeeves (*Tregenseves* 1409), Tregenjeves, '*Cyndefyd's farm*'

Tregonger (*Tregongar* 1453), Tregongar, '*Congar's farm*'

Tregongon (*Tregongan* 1360), Tregongan, '*Congan's farm*'

Tregonhawke (*Trekynheauk* 1357), ?Tregynhavek, ?'*Cynhafoc's farm*'

Tregonhaye (*Tregenhay* 1350), Tregenhay, (?*meaning*)

Tregoniggie (*Tregenegy* 1316), Tregeunegy, '*reed-beds farm*'

Tregonissey (*Tregenedwith* 1224), Tregeneswydh, '*Cyneduit's farm*'

Tregonning (Breage) (*Tregonan* 1341), Tregonan, '*Conan's farm*'

Tregonning (Newlyn East) (Tregonan 1302), Tregonan, '*Conan's farm*'

Tregony (*Trefhrigoni* 1249), Trerygony, '*Rigoni's farm*'

Tregoodwell (*Tregothwal* 1298), Tregothwal, '*Gotual's farm*'

Tregoose (Colan) (*Tregoos* 1410), Tregoos, '*wood farm*'

Tregoose (Probus) (*Tregose* 1523), Tregoos, '*wood farm*'

Tregoose (St Columb) (*Tregose* 1483), Tregoos, '*wood farm*'

Tregoose (St Erth) (*Tregoos* 1523), Tregoos, '*wood farm*'

Tregorrick (*Tregorrek* 1320), Tregorrek, '*Goroc's farm*'

Tregoss (*Tregors* 1210), Tregors, '*reeds farm*'

Tregothnan (*Treguythenan* 1280), Tregwythenan, ?'*Guithenan's farm*'

Tregowris (*Tregeures* 1327), Tregewres, '*hollow-ford farm*'

Tregreenwell (*Tregrenewen* 1338), Tregrenewen, (?*meaning*)

Tregrehan (*Tregrechyon* 1304), Tregryghyon, '*farm of wrinkled fields*'

Tregrill (*Tregrilla* 1284), Tregrylla, '*Crylla's farm*'

Tregullan (*Tregewelen* 1278), Tregewelen, (?*meaning*)

Tregulland (*Tregolan* 1302), Tregolan, '*Colan's farm*'

Tregullow, Tregolow, '*sunlight farm*'

Tregunna (*Tregonow* 1302), Tregonow, '*Conheu's farm*'

Tregunnon (*Gunan* 1189), Goonan, Gonan, '*downland place*'

Tregurrian (*Tregurien* 1232, *Tregorrian* 1699), Tregoryan, '*Coryan's farm*'

Tregurtha (*Tregurthan* 1358), Tregerdhyn, '*rowan-trees farm*'

Tregye (*Tregy* 1327), Tregei/Tregy, '*dog(-breeding) farm*'

Trehan (*Trehanna* 1328), Trehanna, '*Hanna family's farm*'

Trehane (*Treyahan* 1302), Treyahan, '*Iahan's farm*'

Trehemborne (*Trehenben* 1208), Trehenben, '*Henben's farm*'

Treheveras (*Trethyverys* 1379), Tredheverys, '*well-watered farm*'

Trehudreth (*Treiudret* 1201), Treyudreth, '*Iudret's farm*'

Trehunist (*Trenanast* 1327), Trenanast, (?*meaning*)

Trekeivesteps (*Trekyff* 1401), Trekyf, '*tree stump farm*'

Trekelland (Lewannick) (*Trekelryn c.* 1400), Trekelryn, '*farm at a sheltering spur*'

Trekelland (Lezant) (*Trekynmond* 1397), Trekynmond, '*Cynemund's farm*'

Trekenner (Laneast) (*Trekynener* 1244, Trekynener, ?'*Cynener's farm*'

Trekenner (Lezant) (*Tregenner, Trekyner* C13), Tregyner, '*Cynor's farm*'

Trekenning (*Trehepkenyn* 1294), Tre hep Kenyn, *'farm without wild garlic'*

Treknow (*Trenou c.* 1250), Tredenow, *'side-valley farm'*

Trelagossick (*Trelogosek* 1284), Tre logosek, *'mouse-infested farm'*

Trelan (*Trelan* 1288), Trelann, *'enclosure farm'*

Trelash (*Trellosk* 1284), Trelosk, *'farm at burnt/swaled land'*

Trelaske, Trelosk, *'farm at burnt/swaled land'*

Trelassick (*Treloysek* 1345), Treloysek, *'Loidoc's farm'*

Trelavour (*Trelowargh* 1331), Tre lowargh, (?*meaning*)

Trelawne (*Trevelowen* 1284), Trev Elowen, *'elm tree farm'*

Trelawny (*Treleuny* 1175), Treleuny, *'farm on the Leuny stream ('full stream')'*

Trelay (*la Leye* 1305; ME *atte lege*), Atlea, *'at the clearing'*

Treleague (*Trelaek c.* 1300), Trelaeg, *'Leoc's farm'*

Trelease (*Trelys* 1374), Trelys, *'farm by a ruin'*

Treleigh (*Trelegh* 1402), Trelegh, *'slab farm'*

Trelew (Mylor) (*Treleu* 1470), Trelew, *'Leu's farm'*

Trelew (St Buryan) (*Trelywe* 1425), Trelyw, *'farm of colour'*

Treliever (*Trelyver* 1327), Trelyver, *'Lifr's farm'*

Treligga (*Treluga* 1086), Treluga, *'Luga's farm'*

Trelights (*Trefleghtres* 1356), Tre leghtres, ?*'feet-slab (pavement) farm'*

Trelill (Helston) (*Trelulla* 1303), Tre lulla, *'Lulle's farm'*

Trelill (St Breock) (*Trelulla* 1284), Tre lulla, *'Lulla's farm'*

Trelill (St Kew) (*Trelulla* 1262), Tre lulla, *'Lulle's farm'*

Trelion (*Trefleghyon* 1334, *Trelyghon* 1483), Treleghyon, *'slabs farm'*

Treliske (*Trelosk* 1311), Trelosk, *'farm on burnt/swaled land'*

Trelissick (Feock) (*Trelesyk* 1275), Tre lesyk, *'Leidic's farm'*

Trelissick (St Erth) (*Trewelesekwarheil* 1356), Trewolesyk war Heyl, *'Gwledic's farm on the river Hayle'*

Trelissick (St Ewe) (*Trelesik* 1297), Trelesyk, *'Leidic's farm'*

Trelissick (Sithney) (*Trewelesik* 1369), Trewolesyk, *'Gwledic's farm'*

Treliver (*Trelyver* 1340), Trelyver, *'Lifr's farm'*

Treloar (*Trelowarth* 1527), Trelowarth, *'garden farm'*

Trelonk, Trelonk, *'farm by a gully'*

Treloquithack (*Trelaugguethek* 1372), Trelaugwedhek, (?*meaning*)

Trelow (*Trelewyth* 1327), Trelewyth, *'Leuit's farm'*

Trelowarren (*Trelewarent* 1227), Tre lewarent, (?*meaning*)

Trelowia (*Trelewyan* 1303), Trelewyen, *'Leuien's farm'*

Trelowth (*Trelewyth* 1306), Trelewyth, *'Liuit's farm'*

Trelowthas (*Treloudat* 1280), Tre lowdas, *'Leudat's farm'*

Treluggan (Gerrans) (*Trelugan* 1244), Trelugan, *'Lucan's farm'*

Treluggan (Landrake) (*Trelugan* 1346), Trelugan, *'Lucan's farm'*

Treluswell (*Tredutual* 1296), Tre dhuswal, *'Tudwal's farm'*

Tremabyn (*Tremaban* 1327), Tre-mabon, '*Mabon's farm*'

Tremail (*Tremayl* 1284), Tremail, '*Mael's farm*'

Tremaine (*Tremen c.* 1230), Tremen, '*stone farm*'

Tremar (Tremargh 1284), Tremargh, '*horse/March's farm*'

Tremarcoombe (modern), Comm Tremargh, '*valley at Tremar*'

Trematon (*Trementon* 1187), Tremen, '*stone farm* (+ OE *tún*)'

Tremayne (Crowan) (*Tremayn* 1314), Tremeyn, '*stones farm*'

Trembath (*Trenbagh* 1327), Tre'n Bagh, '*farm at the nook/corner*'

Trembethow, Tre'n Bedhow, '*farm at the graves*'

Trembraze (*Trembras* 1338), Tre'n Bras, '*farm of the big man*'

Tremedda or **Tremeader** (*Trevemeder* 1269), Trev Emeder, '*Emeder's farm*'

Tremeer (*Tremuer* 1332), Tremeur, '*great farm*'

Tremelethen (Scilly) (*Tremolefyn* 1310), Tremolefyn, (?*meaning*)

Tremelling (*Tremelyn* 1327), Tre-melyn, '*mill farm*'

Tremenheere (Ludgvan), Tremenhir, '*standing stone farm*'

Tremenheere (Wendron), Tremenhir, '*standing-stone farm*'

Tremenhere (St Keverne), Tremenhir, '*standing-stone farm*'

Tremenhere (Stithians), Tremenhir, '*standing-stone farm*'

Tremethick Cross (*Tremethek* 1284), Tremedhek, '*doctor's farm*'

Tremodrett (*Tremodret* 1086), Tre-modret (OC), '*Modret's farm*'

Tremollett (*Tremollou* 1350), Tre-mollow, (?*meaning*)

Tremore (*Tremhor* 1086), Tre'n Hordh, '*the ram's farm*'

Tremough (*Tremogh* 1366–1590), Tremogh, '*pigs' farm*'

Trenance (Mullion) (*Trenans* 1358), Trenans, '*valley farm*'

Trenance (Newquay) (*Trenans* 1327), Trenans, '*valley farm*'

Trenance (St Keverne) (*Trenans* 1311), Trenans, '*valley farm*'

Trenance (St Mawgan) (*Trenans* 1277), Trenans, '*valley farm*'

Trenance (St Issey) (*Trenans* 1419), Trenans, '*valley farm*'

Trenance (St Wenn) (*Trenans* 1356), Trenans, '*valley farm*'

Trenant (Egloshayle) (*Trenant* 1210), Trenant (OC), '*valley farm*'

Trenant (Fowey) (*Trenansprioris* 1334), Trenans, '*valley farm*'

Trenant (St Neot) (*Trenant* 1449), Trenant (OC), '*valley farm*'

Trenarren (*Tyngaran* 1304), Tingaran, '*crane's/heron's rounded hill*'

Trenarth (*Trenerth* 1262), Trenerth, '*Nerth's farm*'

Trencreek (St Col. Min.) (*Trencruk* 1346), Tre'n Crug, '*farm at the barrow*'

Trencrom (*Trencrom* 1333, *Trecrobum* 1696), Tre'n Crobm, '*farm at the hunch(ed hill)*'

Trendeal (*Tyndel* 1293), Tindel, '*rounded hill with leaves*'

Trendrennen, Tre'n Dreynen, '*farm at the thorn bush*'

Trendrine (*Trendreyn* 1302), Tre'n Dreyn, '*farm at the thorns*'

Treneague (St Stephen) (*Trenanek* 1360), Trenanek, (*?meaning*)

Treneague (Wadebridge) (*Trenahek* 1333), Trenahek, (*?meaning*)

Trenear (Breage) (*Treneyr* 1468), Tre'n Yer, *'the hen's farm'*

Trenear (Wendron) (*Treyner* 1405), Tre'n Yer, *'the hen's farm'*

Treneere (*Trenyer* 1280), Tre'n Yer, *'the hen's farm'*

Treneglos, Tre'n Eglos, *'farm at the church'*

Trenerth (*Trenerth* 1201), Trenerth, *'Nerth's farm'*

Trenethick (*Trevenethek* 1314), Trevenedhek, *'hilly farm'*

Trenewan (*Trenewyen* 1424), Trenewyen, *'Neuyen's farm'*

Trenewth (*Trenewyth* 1296), Trenowyth, *'new farm'*

Trengale (*Trengalla* 1302), Tre'n Galla, *'the Gael's farm'*

Trengilly (*Trengelly* 1309), Tre'n Gelly, *'farm at the grove'*

Trengothal, Tre'n Godhel, *'farm at the watery ground'*

Trengove (*Trengof* 1303), Tre'n Gov, *'the smith's farm'*

Trengrouse (*Trengrous* 1373), Tre'n Grows, *'farm at the cross'*

Trengune (*Trengun* 1356), Tre'n Goon, *'farm at the downs'*

Trengwainton (*Trethigwaynton* 1319), Tredhigwaynton, *'farm of everlasting spring'*

Trenhayle (*Trewarneil* 1302), Tre war Heyl, *'farm on the river Hayle'*

Trenhorne (*Trevenhorn* 1440), Trevenhorn, (*?meaning*)

Treninnick (*Trenynek* 1278), Trenynek, (*?meaning*)

Trenithan (Probus) (*Treneythin* 1259), Tre'n Eythyn, *'farm at the furze'*

Trenithan (St Enoder) (*Treneythin* 1259), Tre'n Eythyn, *'farm at the furze'*

Trenithan Bennett (*Hendrenydyn* 1277), Hendre'n Eythyn, *'Old Trenithan'*

Trennick (*Trewythenek* 1305), Trewydhenek, *'Guithenoc's farm'*

Trenode (*Trenoda c.* 1260), Trenoda, (*?meaning*)

Trenoon (Ruan Major) (*Trevenwoen* 1334), Trev an Woon, *'farm at the downs'*

Trenoon (St Mawgan) (*Trenoen* 1426), Tre'n Woon, *'farm at the downs'*

Trenovissick (*Trenevesek* 1428), Trenevesek, *'farm in a place of sacred groves'*

Trenoweth (Gunwalloe) (*Trenowith* 1486), Trenowyth, *'new farm'*

Trenoweth (Mabe), Trenowyth, *'new farm'*

Trenoweth (St Keverne), Trenowyth, *'new farm'*

Trenoweth (Scilly), Trenowyth, *'new farm'*

Trenowin (*Trenewwyn* 1300), Trenewyn, *'trough farm'*

Trenowth (Grampound Road) (*Trenewyth* 1327), Trenowyth, *'new farm'*

Trenowth (Luxulyan) (*Trenewyth* 1327), Trenowyth, *'new farm'*

Trenowth (St Columb) (*Trenewyth* 1428), Trenowyth, *'new farm'*

Trentinney (*Treventenyu* 1345), Treventynnyow, *'spring-heads farm'*

Trenuggo (*Trewarnogou* 1336), Tre war'n Ogow, *'farm on the cave'*

Trenwheal (Trenuwel 1394), Tre-nuwel, (*?meaning*)

Trenython (*Treneithen* 1201), Tre'n Eythyn, *'farm at the furze'*

Treore (*Treworou* 1281), Treworow, *'Gorou's farm'*

Trequite (St Germans) (*Trequit* 1327), Treguit (OC), *'wood farm'*

Trequite (St Kew) (*Tregoyt* 1331), Treguit (OC), *'wood farm'*

Trereife (*Treruf* 1226), Treruyv (OC), *'king's / Ruyf's farm'*

Trerice (Newlyn East) (*Trereys* 1302–1410), Treres, *'watercourse farm'*

Trerice (St Allen) (*Trereys* 1317–1588), Treres, *'watercourse farm'*

Trerice (Sancreed) (*Trereys* 1424), Treres, *'watercourse farm'*

Treringey (*Trevrengy* 1404), Tre-vrengy, *'Brenci's farm'*

Trerise (*Trereys* 1399), Treres, *'water-course farm'*

Trerulefoot (*Treriwal* 1373), Trerywal, *'Riwal's farm'*

Tresaddern (*Tresoudorn* 1393), Tre-soudorn, *'Soudorn's farm'*

Tresamble (Tresamwell 1277), Tre-samwel, *'Samuel's farm'*

Tresarrett (*Tresiryek* 1305), Tresyriek, (*?meaning*)

Tresavean (*Treyusow vean* C16), Tre-yusow Vian, *'little Treyusow (Iudou's farm)'*

Tresawle (*Tresawel* 1297), Tresawel, *?'Sawel's farm'*

Tresawsan (Merther), Tresowson, *'Englishmen's farm'*

Tresawsen (Perranzabuloe), Tre-sowson, *'Englishmen's farm'*

Trescobeas (*Treskubays* 1356), ?Tre-scubys, *?'swept farm'*

Trescowe (*Trescau* 1283), Trescaw, *'elder-trees farm'*

Tresean (*Tresevion c.* 1200), Tresevien, *'strawberry farm'*

Tresemple (*Tresympel* 1338), Tre-sympel, *'Sympel family's farm'*

Tresevern, Tresevern, *'Saefern's farm'*

Tresillian (*Tresulyan* 1315), Tresulyen, *'Sulyen's farm'*

Tresinney (*Treseny* 1376), Treseny, (*?meaning*)?

Tresithick (*Trevethysek* 1342), Tre-varthusek, *'wonderful farm'*

Treskerby (*Treskirbek* 1393), Tre-skyrbek, (*?meaning*)

Treskillard (*Tresculard* 1327), Tre-scoulard (OC) , *'kite-height farm'*

Treskilling (*Roskelyn* 1356), Roskelyn, *'holly hillspur'*

Treskinnick (*Treskeynek* 1442), Ros-keynek, *'ridge-place roughland'*

Treslay (*Roslegh* 1338), Roslegh, *'slab roughland'*

Treslothan (*Tresulwethen* 1319), Tre-sulwedhen, *'Sulwethen's farm'*

Tresmeer (*Trewasmur* 1185), Trewas-meur, *'Gwasmeur's farm'*

Tresowes (*Tresewys* 1327), Tresewys, *?'stitcher's farm'*

Tresparrett (*Rospervet* 1086), Ros-perveth, *'middle / inner roughland'*

Trespearne (*Trespernan c.* 1200), Tre-spernen, *'thorn tree farm'*

Tresprison (Helston) (*Trespreson* 1327), Tresperysyon, *'farm of spirits'*

Tresprisson (Mullion) (*Trespryson* 1459), Tresperysyon, *'farm of spirits'*

Trestrayle (*Trestrael* 1278), Trestrel, '*mat(-making) farm*'

Tresvennack (*Tresevenek* 1440), Tresevenek, '*Sefenoc's farm*'

Treswithian (*Trevaswethen* 1318), Trevaswedhen, '*Matguethen's farm*'

Tretharrup (St Martin) (*Trewortharap* 1334), Trewortharap, '*very pleasant farm*'

Tretheague (*Trethaec* 1213), Tretheg, '*pretty farm*'

Trethellan (*Trethelyn* 1412; *Tredelyn* 1409), Tredhelyn, '*Delyn's farm*'

Trethem (*Trethrym* 1309), Tredhrumm, '*ridge farm*'

Tretherras (St Columb) (*Tretheyris* 1284), Tretheyrres, '*farm at three fords*'

Tretherres (St Allen) (*tredoures* 1314), Tredhewres, '*farm at two fords*'

Trethevey (Luxulyan) (*Trethewy* 1302), Tredhewy, '*Dewi's farm*'

Trethevey (St Mabyn) (*Tiwardeui* 1201), Ty war Duwy, '*manorial centre on the Dewey river*'

Trethevy (St Cleer) (*Trethewy* 1284), Tredhewy, '*Dewi's farm*'

Trethevy (S. Petherwin) (*Trethewy* 1332), Tredhewy, '*Dewi's farm*'

Trethevy (Tintagel) (*Trethewy* 1306), Tredhewy, '*Dewi's farm*'

Trethew (*Trethu c.* 1120), Tredhu, '*black / dark farm*'

Trethewell (*Trethiwol* 1342), Tredhywal, '*Dywal's farm*'

Trethewey (Germoe) (*Trethewy* 1327), Tredhewy, '*Dewi's farm*'

Trethewey (St Ervan) (*Trethewy* 1286), Tredhewy, '*Dewi's farm*'

Trethewey (St Levan) (*Trethewy* 1320), Tredhewy, '*Dewi's farm*'

Trethewey (St Martin) (*Trethewy* 1371), Tredhewy, '*Dewi's farm*'

Trethill (*Treyuthell* 1393), Treyudhal, '*Iudhael's farm*'

Trethillick (*Treworthelek* 1284), Trewordhelek, '*Gortheloc's farm*'

Trethingey (*Trethingey* 1259), Tredhinegy, '*farm by fortified places*'

Trethosa (*Trewythoda* 1327), Trewythosa, ?'*Guithoda's farm*'

Trethowel (St Austell) (*Trethywall* 1345), Tredhywal, '*Dywal's farm*'

Trethowell (Kea) (*Treworthual* 1302), Treworthawel, '*very quiet farm*'

Trethurffe (*Trederveu c.* 1200), ?Tredherva, ?'*oak wood farm*'

Trethurgy (*Trethevergy* 1251), Tredhevergy, '*Dofergi's farm*'

Trevadlock (*Trevathelek* 1440), Trevathelek, '*Mateloc's farm*'

Trevales (*Trevatheles* 1356), Trev Edhelys, '*farm at a place of aspens*'

Trevalga (*Trevalga* 1238), Trevalga, '*Maelga's farm*'; (*Menaliden c.* 1150), Mene'ledan, '*wide hillside*'

Trevalgan (*Trevaelgon* 1320), Trevalgon, '*Maelgon's farm*'

Trevalso (*Trevalda c.* 1310), Trevalsa, '*Maelda's farm*'

Trevance (*Trevantros* 1201), Trevantros (OC), '*farm at a hollow hillspur*'

Trevanger (*Trevangar* 1284), Trev Angar, ?'*Ancar / hermit's farm*'

Trevanion (*Trevenyon* 1326), Trev Enyon, '*Enion's farm*'

Trevanson (*Trevansun* 1259), Trev Ansun, '*Antun's farm*'

Trevarnon (*Treveranon* 1370), Treveranon, '*Meranon's farm*'

Trevarrack (Penzance) (*Treverek* 1284), Treverek, *'Meroc's farm'*

Trevarrack (St Ives) (*Trevorek* 1284), Trevorek, *'Moroc's farm'*

Trevarren (*Treveren* 1244), Treveren, *'Meren's farm'*

Trevarrian (*Treveryon* 1345), Treveryen, *'Merien's farm'*

Trevarrick (*Trevarthek* 1332), Trev Arthek, *'Arthoc's farm'*

Trevarth (*Trevargh* 1277), Trevargh, *'horse/March's farm'*

Trevaskis (Gwinear) (*Trevalscus* 1523), Trevalscus, *'Maelscuit's farm'*

Trevaunance (*Trefuunans* 1302), Trevawnans, *'beech valley farm'*

Trevaylor (*Treveller* 1245), Trevelor, *'Melor's farm'*

Treveal (Cubert) (*Trevael* 1291), Trevail, *'Mael's farm'*

Treveal or **Trevail** (Towednack) (*Trevael* 1327), Trevail, *'Mael's farm'*

Trevean (Kea), Trevian, *'little farm'*

Trevean (Madron), Trevian, *'little farm'*

Trevean (Morvah), Trevian, *'little farm'*

Trevean (Newlyn East), Trevian, *'little farm'*

Trevean (Perranuthnoe), Trevian, *'little farm'*

Trevean (Sancreed), Trevian, *'little farm'*

Trevean (St Keverne), Trevian, *'little farm'*

Trevean (St Levan), Trevian, *'little farm'*

Trevean (St Merryn), Trevian, *'little farm'*

Trevear (St Issey), Treveur, *'great farm'*

Trevear (St Merryn), Treveur, *'great farm'*

Trevear (Sennen), Treveur, *'great farm'*

Trevedra (*Treverdreth, Trewardraght* 1668), Tre war Dreth, *'farm on a beach'*

Trevedran (*Trewydren* 1284), Trewydren, *'Guidren's farm'*

Trevega or **Trevessa** (*Trevysa* 1507), Trevija, *'lowest farm'*

Trevegean (*Trevegyon* 1297), Trevujyon, *'chaff farm'*

Treveglos, Trev Eglos, *'churchtown'*

Treveighan (*Trevegon* 1338), Trevegon, (*?meaning*)

Treveighan (*Trevegon* 1309, *Trevygan* 1461), Trevygan, (*?meaning*)

Trevelgue (*Trevelgy* 1284), Trevailgy, *'Maelgi's farm'*

Trevellas (*Trevelles* 1302), Treveles, *'Meled's farm'*

Trevelmond (ME *atte* + F *bel mont*), Atbelmont, *'at the fair hill'*

Trevelver (*Trevelvargh* 1219), Trev Almargh, *'Aelmarch's farm'*

Trevemedor (*Trevemeder* 1208), Trev Emeder, *'Emeder's farm'*

Trevemper (*Trevymper* 1360), Trevymper, (*?meaning*)

Treven (Tintagel) (E, *atte Fenne* 1317), Atfen, *'at the marsh'*

Trevena (Breage) (*Tremuno* 1318, *Trevuno* 1436), Trevuno, (*?meaning*)

Trevena (Tintagel) (*Trewarvene* 1259), Tre war Vene', Tre war Veneth *'farm on a hillside'*

Treveneague (*Trevanahek* 1356), Trevanahek, *'monastic farm'*

Trevenen (*Trevaenwyn* 1310), Trevenwynn, *'white stone farm'*

Trevenen Bal, Bal Trevenwynn, *'mine at Trevenen'*

Trevennen (Goran) (*Trevenyen* 1393), Trev Enyan, *'Enian's farm'*

Treveor, Treveur, *'large farm'*

Treverbyn (St Austell) (*Treverbin* 1086), Trev Erbyn, *'Erbin's farm'*

Treverbyn (St Neot) (*Treverbyn* 1284), Trev Erbyn, *'Erbin's farm'*

Treverva (*Trefurvo* 1358), Trev Urvo, ?*'Urvo's farm'*

Treverven (*Treverwyn* 1380), Treverwyn, *'Berwyn's farm'*

Trevescan (*Trefescan* 1302), Trevhesken, *'sedge farm'*

Trevethan (Falmouth) (*Trefuthen* 1327), Trevudhyn, *'meadow farm'*

Trevethan (Gwennap) (*Trefuthyn c.* 1516), Trevudhyn, *'meadow farm'*

Trevethow, Trevedhow, *'farm by graves'*

Trevia (*Trewya* 1272), Trewia, *'weaving farm'*

Trevider (*Trevehether* 1500), Treworheder, *'Gorheder's farm'*

Treviglas, Trev Eglos, *'churchtown'*

Trevigro (*Trefigerow* 1327), Trev Egerow, *'openings farm'*

Trevilder (*Treveleder* 1284), Trev Eleder, *'Eleder's farm'*

Treviles (*Trevaelus* 1293), Trevalos, *'Maelod's farm'*

Trevilla (*Trewilla* 1086) (OE, *æt þæm wiella*), Atwell, *'at the stream/spring'*

Trevillador (*Treveleder* 1327), Trev Eleder, *'Eleder's farm'*

Trevillett (*Trevellet* 1338), Trevelet (OC), *'vermillion farm'*

Trevilley (St Columb) (*Trevely* 1302), Trevely, *'Beli's farm'*

Trevilley (St Teath) (*Treveli* 1201), Trevely, *'Beli's farm'*

Trevilley (Sennen) (*Trevelly* 1296), Trevely, *'Beli's farm'*

Trevilson (*Trevelson* 1293), Trevelson, (?*meaning*)

Trevine (*Trebyghan* 1296), Trevian, *'small farm'*

Treviscoe (*Tref otcere* 1049, *Trevyskar* 1327), Trev Osker, *'Otcer's farm'*

Treviskey (Gwennap) (*Trevrysky* 1404), Trevrysky, *'Britci's farm'*

Treviskey (Veryan) (*Trevythky* 1332), Trevythky, (?*meaning*)

Trevisquite (*Treveskoyd* 1306), Trev ys Cuit (OC), *'farm below a wood'*

Trevithal (*Trevethegal* 1315), Trevedhegel, *'surgery farm'*

Trevithick (St Columb) (*Treweythek* 1392), Treweythek, (?*meaning*)

Trevithick (St Ewe) (*Trevethik* 1303), Trevudhek, *'Budoc's farm'*

Trevivian (*Trefyuian* 1301), Trev Ewen, *'yew-tree farm'*

Trevoll (*Treroval* 1345), Treroval, (?*meaning*)

Trevolland (*Trevolghan* 1338), Trevolghen, *'farm at a small gap'*

Trevone (Mabe) (*Trevouhan* 1343), Trev Ohen, *'oxen farm'*

Trevone (Padstow) (*Treavon* 1302), Trevon, *'mineral farm'*

Trevorder (*Trewordre* 1284), Trewordre, *'farm on a principal estate'*

Trevorgans (*Treworgans* 1356), Treworgans, *'Uuorcant's farm'*

Trevorian (Sennen) (*Treveryan* 1296), Treveryan, *'Beriana's farm'*

Trevorian (Sancreed) (*Treverthion* 1384), Treverghyon, *'Meirchyon's farm'*

Trevornick (*Trefornek c.* 1350), Trefornek, *'bake-house farm'*

Trevorrian (St Buryan) (*Treworyan* 1323), Treworyan, *'Uuorien's farm'*

Trevorrick (St Issey) (*Treworrec* 1277), Treworek, '*Goroc's farm*'

Trevorrick (St Merryn) (*Treworrech* C13), Treworek, '*Goroc's farm*'

Trevorrow (*Treworveu* 1299), Treworvow, '*Gorvo's farm*'

Trevose (*Trenfos* 1302), Tre'n Vos, '*farm at the wall/bank*'

Trevowah (*Trevewa* 1290), Trev Ewa, '*Ewa's farm*'

Trevowhan (*Treveuan* 1283), Trev Ewan, '*Ewan's farm*'

Trew (Breage) (*Trethu* 1284), Tredhu, '*black/dark farm*'

Trew (Tresmeer) (*Treuf c.* 1250), Treyuv, '*Yuf's farm*'

Trewalder (*Trewaleder* 1280), Trewaleder, '*Gwaleder's farm*'

Trewan (*Treiowan* 1327), Treyowan, '*Ieuan's farm*'

Trewardale (*Trevertal* 1201), Tre war Dal, '*farm on a hill-brow*'

Trewardreva (*Trewodreve* 1303), Trewodrevy, '*homesteads farm*'

Trewarlett (*Trewalred* 1308), Trewalred (OC), '*Walred's farm*'

Trewarmett (*Trewerman* 1302), Trewerman, '*Germanus's farm*'

Trewarnevas (*Treworneves* 1302), Treworneves, '*Gorneved's farm*'

Trewartha (Merther) (*Treworou* 1327), Treworow, '*Gorou's farm*'

Trewartha (St Agnes) (*Andrewartha c.* 1720), an Drewartha, '*the higher farm*'

Trewartha (St Neot), ?Trewartha, ?'*higher farm*'

Trewartha (Veryan), Trewartha, '*higher farm*'

Trewarthenick (*Trewethenec* 1326), Trewedhenek, '*Guethenoc's farm*'

Trewarveneth, Tre war Veneth, '*farm on a hillside*'

Trewashford (ME) *atte*, (OE) *wæsce ford*), Atwashford, '*at the wash-place ford*'

Trewassa (Trewasa 1284), Trewasa, '*Gata's farm*'

Trewavas, Trewavos, '*winter-dwelling farm*'

Treween (*Trewoen* 1356), Trewoon, '*downs farm*'

Trewellard (*Trewylard* 1327), Trewylard, '*Gwylard's farm*'

Trewen (Camelford) (*Trewenna* 1301), Trewenna, '*farm on the Wenna stream (fair one)*'

Trewen (Trewen) (*Trewen* 1289), Trewynn, '*white/fair farm*'

Trewennack (*Trewethenek* 1296), Trewedhenek, '*Guethenoc's farm*'

Trewennan (*Trewynan* 1347), Trewynen, '*Guinen's farm*'

Trewern (*Treyouran* 1302), Treyouren, '*Youren's farm*'

Trewetha (*Treweyther* 1426), Trewyther, '*Gwythyr's farm*'

Trewethan (*Trewythian* 1327), Trewydhyan, '*Guidien's farm*'

Trewether (*Trewydyr* 1294), Trewydhyr, '*Gwythyr's farm*'

Trewethern (*Trewotheran* C14, *Trewodren* C15) Trewodhren, '*Godren's farm*'

Trewethert (*Trewythred* 1306), Trewythred (OC), '*Gwythred's farm*'

Trewey (*Trethewy* 1314), Tredhewy, '*Dewi's farm*'

Trewhella (*Trewhyla* 1357), Trewhila, '*beetle-infested farm*'

Trewhiddle (*Trewydel* 1262), Trewydel (OC), ?'*Guidal's farm/tree-place farm*'

Trewidden, Trewydn, '*white/fair farm*'

Trewidland (*Trewythelan* 1298), Trewydhelan, '*Gwydelan's farm*'

Trewince (Stithians) (*Trewins* 1584), Trewyns, '*wind(y) farm*'

Trewince (St Columb), Trewyns, '*wind(y) farm*'

Trewince (St Issey) (*Trewyns* 1348), Trewyns, '*wind(y) farm*'

Trewince (Scilly) (*Trewins* 1650), Trewyns, '*wind(y) farm*'

Trewindle (*Trewynell* 1570), Trewynnel, '*white stream farm*'

Trewinnard (*Trewynard* 1319), Trewynard, '*Guinart's farm*'

Trewint (Altarnun) (*Trewynt* 1324), Trewynt (OC), '*wind(y) farm*'

Trewint (Blisland) (*Tyrwint c.* 1510), Tirwynt (OC), '*wind(y) land*'

Trewint (Poundstock) (*Trewynt* 1300), Trewynt (OC), '*wind(y) farm*'

Trewirgie (Probus) (*Trewythgi* 1298), Trewydhgy, '*Guidci's farm*'

Trewirgie (Redruth) (*Trewythgy* 1334), Trewydhgy, '*Guidci's farm*'

Trewithen (*Trewythyan* 1337), Trewydhyen, '*Guidien's farm*'

Trewithian (*Trewythyan c.* 1270), Trewydhyen, '*Guidien's farm*'

Trewollack (Gorran) (*Trewolak* 1426), Trewolak, (*?meaning*)

Trewoodloe (ME *atte wode*) + *river name*), Atwood Logh, '*at the wood by river Looe*'

Trewoofe (*Trewoyf* 1302, Trewofe 1668), Trewav, '*winter farm*'

Trewoon (Mullion), Trewoon, '*downs farm*'

Trewoon (St Mewan), Trewoon, '*downs farm*'

Treworga (*Treworge* 1314), Treworge, '*low/broken hedge farm*'

Treworgan (Mawnan) (*Trewothgan* 1338), Trewodhgen, '*Goethgen's farm*'

Treworgans (Cubert) (*Treworgans* 1327), Treworgans, '*Gorcant's farm*'

Treworgans (Probus) (*Treworgans* 1354), Treworgans, '*Gorcant's farm*'

Treworgey (Duloe) (*Treworgy* 1365), Treworgy, '*Wurci's farm*'

Treworgey (Liskeard) (*Treworgy* 1385), Treworgy, '*Wurci's farm*'

Treworgie (Manaccan) (*Treworgy* 1323), Treworgy, '*Wurci's farm*'

Treworlas (*Treworlas* 1327), Treworlas, '*Gorlas's farm*'

Treworld (*Treworwel* 1288), Treworwel, '*Gorwel's farm*'

Trewornan (*Tregronan* 1303), Trewreunen, '*grain farm*'

Treworrick (*Treworek* 1302), Treworek, '*Goroc's farm*'

Treworthal (*Trewoethel* 1292), Trewodhel, '*farm on watery ground*'

Trewrickle (*Trewikkel c.* 1190), Trewykel, '*farm at a small forest settlement*'

Treyarnon (*Treyarnen c.* 1250), Treyarnen, '*Iarnen's farm*'

Trezaise (*Treseys* 1302), Treseys, '*Englishman's farm*'

Trezare (*Reswor* 1302), ?Reswor, (*?meaning*)

Trezelah, Treseghla, '*dry-place farm*'

Trink (*Trefrynk* 1333), Trefrynk, '*Frenchman's/freeman's farm*'

Trispen (*Tredespan* 1325), Tredhespan, '*Despan's farm*'

Troan (*Treiowen* 1327), Treyowan, '*Ieuan's farm*'

Troon (Camborne) (*Trewoen* 1327), Trewoon, '*downs farm*'

Troswell (*Treswell* 1249; OE, *tréowes wielle*), Treeswell, '*spring by trees*'

Trowan (*Trevowan* 1327), Trev Ohen, '*oxen farm*'

Truas (*Trewys* 1304), Trewis, '*sow's farm*'

Trungle (*Trevonglet* 1283), Trevongleudh, '*farm at an open-cast mine*'

Truro (*Tryveru* 1264), Triverow, Truru, ?'*three turbulent streams*'

Truscott (*Troscote* 1327) Troscuit (OC), '*beyond a wood*'

Trussall (*Trewrosel* 1327), Trewrosel, (?*meaning*)

Truthall (*Treuthal* 1281), Treyudhal, '*Iudhael's farm*'

Truthwall (Crowan) (*Trewothwal* 1356), Trewodhwal, '*Godual's farm*'

Truthwall (Ludgvan) (*Treuthal* 1086), Treyudhal, '*Iudhael's farm*'

Truthwall (St Just) (*Trewothwall* 1495), Trewodhwal, '*Godual's farm*'

Trye (*Trevry* 1325), Trevry, '*Fri's farm*'

Trythall (*Trewreythel* 1289), Trewreythyel, '*farm where root crops grow*'

Trythance (*Treyuthgans* 1330), Treyudhgans, '*Iudcant's farm*'

Trythogga (*Tredoga* 1310), Tredhoga, '*Doga's farm*'

Tuckingmill (Camborne) (*Talgarrek* 1260), Talgarrek, '*hill-brow rock*'

Tuckingmill (E, *St Breward* C18), Tucking Mill, '*fulling mill*'

Tucoyse (Constantine), (*Tucoys c.* 1240), Tucoos, '*side-wood*'

Tucoyse (St Ewe) (*Tucoys* 1428), Tucoos, '*side-wood*'

Tutwell (E, *Tudewille* 1337), Tudwell, '*Tuda's spring/stream*'

Twelveheads (E), Twelve Heads, '*twelve-headed stamping mill*'

Two Bridges (E), Two Bridges, '*two bridges*'

Two Burrows (E), Two Barrows, '*two barrows*'

Twowatersfoot (E), Twowatersfoot, '*foot of two streams*'

Tywardreath (*Tywardrait c.* 1150), Ty war Dreth, '*manorial centre at a beach/ferry*'

Tywarnhayle, Ty war'n Heyl, '*manorial centre by tidal flats*'

Upton (Bude) (*Uppaton* 1206; OE, *uppe tún*), Upperton, '*higher farm*'

Upton (Linkinhorne) (*Uppatun* 1394), Upperton, '*higher farm*'

Upton Towans (*Andrewartha* 1586), Tewyn an Drewartha, '*sand dunes at an Drewartha*'

Valley Truckle (*Velyntrukky* n.d.), Melyn Droghya, '*tucking (fulling) mill*'

Varfell (*Varwell* 1568), Varwell, '*Varwell family*'

Velanewson (*Vellanusen* 1748), Melyn Usyon, '*the chaff mill*'

Vellandreath, Melyn Dreth, '*beach mill*'

Vellandruchar, Melyn Droghya, '*tucking (fulling) mill*'

Vellandruchia (*Mellintrucke* 1652), Melyn Droghya, '*tucking (fulling) mill*'

Vellanoweth (Ludgvan) (*Melynnoweth* 1520), Melyn Nowyth, '*new mill*'

Vellansagia (*Melyn Saya* 1590), Melyn Saya, '*sifting mill*'

Vellynsaundry, Melyn Sandry, '*Sandry family's mill*'

Venterdon (Cor, E, *Fentendon* 1337), Fenten, '*spring/well*'

Venton Ariance, Fenten Arhans, *'silver well'*

Ventonarren (*Fentenworen* 1548), Fenten Woron, *'St Goron's well'*

Ventonear, Fenten Ia, *'St Ia's well'*

Ventongassic (*Fontenkadoc* 1223), Fenten Gasek, *'St Cadoc's well'*

Ventongimps (*Fentongempes* 1296), Fenten Gompes, *'spring in a level place'*

Ventonglidder (*Fentengleder* 1327), Fenten Gledher, *'St Cleder's well'*

Ventonlassick (*Fentenlageck* 1311), Fenten Lajek, *'St Ladoca's well'*

Ventonleague (*Ventenlegh* 1499), Fenten Legh, *'slab well'*

Ventonraze (*Fyntenras* 1388), Fenten Ras, *'grace well'*

Ventontrissick (*Ventondrissick* 1766), Fenten Dreysek, *'brambly spring'*

Venton Vaise (*Funtenvaes* 1311), Fenten Vas, *'shallow spring'*

Ventonvedna (*Fenton venna* 1303), Fenten Vedna, *'overflowing spring'*

Ventonveth (*Vyntonvergh* 1370), Fenten Vergh, *'horses' spring'*

Venton Vision, Fenten Vesen, *'acorn well'*

Ventonwyn (Creed) (*Fentenwyn* 1370), Fenten Wynn, *'white/fair spring'*

Ventonwyn (St Stephen) (*Fentenwyn* 1442), Fenten Wynn, *'white/fair spring'*

Venwyn (*Menven* 1327, *Venwin* 1659), Menwynn, *'white stone'*

Veryan (*Elerghy* 1349), Elerhy, *'place of swans'*

Victoria (E, C19), Victoria, (*inn name*)

Viscar (*Fursgore* 1290; OE, *fyrs gára*), Furzegar, *'furze corner'*

Vogue (*Voss* 1603), an Vos, *'the wall/dwelling'*

Vogue Beloth (*Vogue Bellow* 1945), an Vos Pella, *'the further Vogue'*

Vorvas or **Worvas** (*Gorvos* 1258), Gorvos, *'high dwelling'*

Vose (*la Vos* 1301), Fos, *'wall/bank'*

Voskelly, Foskelly, *'wall/bank by a grove'*

Vounder (St Blazey) (*Vounder* 1743), an Vownder, *'the lane/droveway'*

Vounder (Mullion) (*Bonder* 1286, *Vounder* 1564), Bownder, *'lane/droveway'*

Wadebridge (*Wade* 1312; OE, *wæd*), Wade, *'ford'*

Wainhouse Corner (*Wynehous* 1440), Winehouse, *'wine house'*

Wall (E, *Walle* 1457), Wall, *'wall'*

Wanson (*Wansand* 1308; OE, *wann sand*), Wansand, *'dark sand'*

Warbstow (*S. Werburge* c. 1180), Werburgh, *'St Waerburh'*

Warleggan (*Worlegan* c. 1260), ?Worlegan, ?*'watchplace'*

Washaway (E), Washway, *'washed-out way'*

Watergate (Advent) (E), Watergate, *'sluice gate'*

Watergate (Pelynt) (E), Watergate, *'sluice gate'*

Water-ma-Trout (E), Wet-my-throat, *(for a dry field)*

Wearde (*Werde* 1337; OE, *weard*), Ward, *'watch (place)'*

Week St Mary (*Wyk* 1284; OE, *wíc*), Wyk, *'dairy farm'*

Weeth (*The Weath* 1677), an Wydh, *'the trees'*

Welltown (*Wylton* 1565), Welltown, *'well/spring farm'*

Wendron (*Egloswendron* 1513), Eglos Wendern, *'St Gwendern's church'*; (*Eglosiga* 1208), Eglos Syga, *'Siga's church'*

Wenford Bridge (*Wennford Bridge* 1613) (E), Ryswenn, *'ford on the river Gwenn'*

Werrington (OE, *Ulvredintone* 1086), Wulfredington, *'farm of Wulfred's people'*

West Carne (*Westcarn* 1350), Carn West, *'western Carn'*

Westcott (OE, *Westecote* 1340), Westcot, *'western cottage'*

West Curry (*Great Cory* 1748), Cory Veur, *'great Cory'*

West Looe (*Porthbighan* 1280), Porth Bian, *'small cove/harbour'*

West Pentire (*Pentir c.* 1270), Pentir, *'promontory'*

West Tolgus (*Talgoys Vian* 1485), Talgos Vian, *'little Tolgus'*

Westway (*Westva* 1659), Gwestva, *'lodging house'*

Whalesborough (OE, *Wéales bréw*), Walesbrow, *'Celt's hill-brow'*

Wheal Bal (*Whele an Bal* 1780), Whel an Bal, *'mine works at the diggings'*

Wheal Buller (Redruth), Whel Buller, *'Buller family's mine'*

Wheal Buller (St Just) (*Goonevas* 1841), Goon Havos, *'shieling downs'*

Wheal Jane, ?Whel Yeyn, ?*'cold mine'* (or personal name *Jane*)

Wheal Kitty, Whel Kitty, *'Kitty's mine'*

Wheal Owles, Whel Als, *'cliff mine'*

Wheal Reeth, Whel Rudh, *'red mine'*

Wheal Rose, Whel Ros, *'roughland mine'*

Wheal Vlow, Whel Vlou, *'blue mine'*

Wheal Vor, Whel Vor', *'road mine'*

Wheatley (*Wyteleye* 1327; OE, *hwít léah*), Whitelea, *'white/fair clearing'*

Wherry Town (E), Wherry Town, *'wherry (type of boat) settlement'*

White Cross (Cury) (*Crous* 1289), Crows, *'cross'*

White Cross (St Columb Major) (E), White Cross, *'white cross'*

Whitecross (Ludgvan) (E, C18), White Cross, *'white cross'*

Whitecross (Wadebridge) (E, C18), White Cross, *'white cross'*

Whitecross (Lanteglos by Fowey) (E, C19), White Cross, *'white cross'*

Whiteleigh (*Whitelegh* 1345; OE, *hwít léah*), Whitelea, *'white/fair clearing'*

Whitemoor (St Dennis) (E, C18), White Moor, *'white/fair marsh'*

Whitewell (St Teath) (E, C19), White Well, *'white/fair spring'*

Whitstone (OE, *hwít stán*), Whitestone, *'white stone'*

Wicca (*Wicke* 1545) Wyk, *'(farm of the) de Wykke family'*

Widegates (*Widegate* 1748), Widegate, *'wide gate'*

Widemouth Bay (OE, *wídan múða*), Widemouth, *'wide gap in the cliffs'*

Wilcove (E), Well Cove, *'cove by a well'*

Winnards Perch (E), Winnard's Perch, *'redwing's perch'*

Winnianton (*Gwynyon* 1439), Gwynnan, *'white/fair place'*

Winnick (Pentewan) (*The Winnick c.* 1810), an Wynnek, *'the white one (stream name)'*

Winnick (St Veep) (*Guenneck* 1327), Gwynnek, *'white one (stream name)'*

Withiel (*Guythiel-Eglos* 1357), Eglos Wydhyel, *'church at a place of trees'*

Withielgoose (*Wythiell Goyse* 1549), Gwydhyel Goos, *'wood at Withiel'*

Withielgoose Mills (*Goose Mill* 1616), Melyn Goos, *'wood mill'*

Woodford (Morwenstow) (OE, *wudu ford*), Woodford, '*ford by a wood*'

Woolley (*Wullegh* 1493; OE, *wulfa léah*), Wolflea, '*wolf's clearing*'

Woolston (Poundstock) (*Ulnodestone* 1086), Wolfnothston, '*Wulfnoth's farm*'

Woolston (St Ive) (*Ullavestone* 1086), Wulflafeston, '*Wulflafe's farm*'

Woon (*Guoyn* 1335), Goon, '*downs*'

Worthyvale (*Guerdevalan* 1086), Gwarthavalen, '*above an apple tree*'

Worvas or **Vorvas** (*Gorvos* 1258), Gorvos, '*high dwelling*'

Wringford (OE, *Wringworthi* 1299), Wringworthy, '*cheese-press farm*'

Wringworthy (OE, *Wryngeworthy* 1294), Wringworthy, '*cheese-press farm*'

Yeolmbridge (E, *Yambrigge* c. 1250), Yambridge, '*bridge over the river Yam*'

Yeolmouth (OE, *géol múða*), Yel Mouth, '*mouth of a chasm*'

Yolland (*Oldelande* 1377), Oldland, '*old land/holding*'

Youlstone (Morwenstow) (OE, *Yulkesdone* 1302), Yolksdon, '*Geoloc's hill*'

Youlstone (Warbstow) (*Yoldeton* 1326), Oldton, '*old farm*'

Zelah (Sele 1311) (OE *sele*), Sele, '*hall*'

Zennor (*Egglose Zennor* 1561, *Eglos Senor* 1869), Eglos Senar, Eglos Zenar, '*St Senara's church*'

Zoar (C18), Zoar, (*Biblical name*)

Some common place-name elements

A selection of the most common words found in Cornish place names is provided below. These are only given as a general guide but also show some of the variant spellings found in their current forms. Variants that are underlined show the archaic Old Cornish forms that survive particularly in eastern Cornish names, while those in brackets show characteristics of Late Cornish. In this list, masculine nouns are unmarked, and *f.* denotes feminine nouns and the rare feminine form of an adjective.

Cornish	*Traditional forms*
als *f.*	**alt**, **halt**, **hault**, als, alls, halls, owles
	cliff, coast, slope
an	*an, a, y*
	the
an	*an, en*
	of the, at the
bal	*bal*
	diggings (usually at a mine)
bian	*byan, bean, vean, -pean, -pian, biggan, biffin*
	little, small
bos	**bod**, **bot**, *bos, bo, (boj)*
	dwelling (often followed by a person's name)
bre *f.*	*brea, bray, -vrea, -fra, -vra, -frey*
	hill
bron	*burn, brown, barn, borne*
	hill
bugh *f.*	*bew, bow, bu, bue*
	cow
carn	*carn, carne, -garn, -garne*
	tor, crag
carrek *f.*	*carrick, carrack, garrick, garrack*
	rock
chy, **ty**	**ty**, *chy, chi, che, ch'*
	house

compes — *gumpus, gumpas, gimps*
level, even, flat

coos — ***cuit, quite, cote, cott, cut,*** *coys, coose, goose, cus*
a wood

coth — *coath, goath, cooth*
old

crows *f.* — *crows, crowz, grouse, growse*
a cross

crug — *creek, crug, creeg, creak, greek, crig, creg, creege*
barrow, tumulus, mound

du — *due, dhu, thew, sue, diu, dew, jew*
black, dark

din, dinas — *dennis, deen, dun, den, dinnis, dem, dine, dom*
hill fort, cliff castle

eglos *f.* — *eglos, iglas*
church

-ek, -ak — *-ick, -ack, -eck, - ec, -ock*
adjectival suffix, often denoting where something
is found or grows

enys *f.* — *enys, ennis, innis, ince, ennys*
island, isolated or remote place

fenten *f.* — *fenton, venton, venta, fenter*
a natural spring or well

fordh *f.* — *fr', for, vor, forth, fore*
road, way

fos *f.* — *vose, voes, voss, vos*
wall, dyke, bank, rampart

glas — *glaze, glase, las, laze, lase*
green, blue, grey

godrev *f.* — *godrevy, godreva* (plurals)
homestead

goles — *gollas, wollas, gullas*
lower, bottom

goon, gon- *f.* — *goon, goen, guen, gun, gon, woon, noon, un, oon, woone*
downs, open moorland

gwartha — *gwartha, wartha*
higher, upper

gwel — *gweal, gwel, gul, gold, gal*
open field (a similar word, **gwel** *f.*, means 'view')

gwynn, gwydn	*gwin, wyn, win, gwen f., gwidden, widden, quidden, wedden f.*	
	white, fair (rarely, 'holy')	
hal *f.*	*hal, hale*	
	marsh, moor	
hen	*hen*	
	old, ancient	
heyl	*hayle, hel, hele, hyl*	
	estuary/inlet with tidal flats	
hir	*heer, here, heere, hire*	
	long, tall	
kelly *f.*	*killy, kelly, gelly, gilly, calle, col, colli, killi, cold*	
	grove, copse	
ker *f.*	*ker, caer, car, gear, care, gare, cr', gr', cair, caire*	
	fort, ancient enclosed farm	
keyn, kyl	*kine, kil, cein, can, kel, ten*	
	back, ridge (another word **kyl** means 'nook, recess')	
lann, ladn, lan- *f.*	*lan, la, lam, land, le*	
	early enclosed church site (often followed by a saint's or other personal name. Some **lan** names actually contain **nans**, 'valley')	
leyn *f.*	*leen, lin, lane, lene*	
	stitch of land, strip field	
logh *f.*	*loe, looe, lo, low, lu, lowe*	
	deep water inlet/estuary	
loos, los-	**lud, lid, lot,** *looz, loose, lews*	
	grey	
lynn, lydn *f.*	*lyn, land, linn, le, lan, lin, (lidden)*	
	pool, pond	
lys, les *f.*	*lis, les, lease, leaze, las*	
	court, ruin, administrative centre	
margh	*marth, mare, mark, mar*	
	horse	
marhas *f.*	*maraz*	
	market	
melen	*mellyn, melling, mellan, vellan, vellen*	
	yellow (this can be easily confused with **melyn**, below)	
melyn *f.*	*mellyn, melling, mellan, vellan, vellyn, mellen, mellin, mellon*	
	mill	
men	*men, maen, mayne, meyne, ven, van, maine*	
	stone (some names may contain the plural **meyn**)	

meneth, mene'   *mena, mennor, menor, venna, vena, venner, veneth*
       hill, hillside

meur   *mear, meor, veor, meer, vear, mere*
       great, large

nans   ***nant*, *lant*, *nett*,** *nans, nance, niss, nas, ness, lan, lam, nan*
       valley

nowyth   *noweth, nouth, nowth, newth, nowah, nuth, nute*
       new

park   *park, parc*
       field

penn, pedn, pen-   *penn, pedn*
       head, headland, end, top

pentir   *pentire*
       headland, promontory

pol   *pol, poll, bol, pool, pull*
       pool, pond, pit, cove, creek

pons   ***pont*,** *pons, ponds, pon*
       bridge

porth   *porth, por, pr', par*
       cove, landing place, harbour, gateway, entrance

pras   *praze*
       meadow

res, rys *f.*   ***red*, *rid*, *ret*, *rit*,** *res, rice, tres, re, rase, reise, rose, rease*
       ford

res   *res, race, rose, rice*
       watercourse (this can be confused with **res**, above)

ros *f.*   *ros, rose, roose, rowse, tres, ras, res*
       roughland, hillspur, coastal slope, promontory,
       uncultivated valley

sans   ***sant*, *zant*, *sent*,** *zance, sens, sence*
       holy, sacred

sawen *f.*   *zawn, saun, sowan, zone*
       coastal chasm or cleft

segh   *seath, zeath, sig, zeth, shea*
       dry, waterless

tewyn   *towan, tewan*
       sand dunes

toll   *tol, toll, tole*
       hole (can also mean "tithe
       boundary")

tonn, **todn** *ton, don, todn, todden, dodnan*
grassland, turf, pastureland

tre, trev *f.* *tre, trev, -dre, -dra, -drea*
farm, settlement

treth *treath, dreath, -dra*
sand, beach

war *war, ver, var*
on, upon

whel *wheal, huel*
mine workings

yeyn *jane, ine, eyn, yon*
cold, bleak

yn, y'n *en, in, 'n*
in, in the

Lightning Source UK Ltd.
Milton Keynes UK
UKOW04f1412160118
316245UK00001B/55/P

9 781904 808220